712

The English Formal Garden

Günter Mader
Laila Neubert–Mader

The English Formal Garden

Five Centuries of Design

Aurum Press

To our children, Hannah and Florian

This English language edition first published in Great Britain 1997
by Aurum Press Ltd, 25 Bedford Avenue, London WC1B 3AT

Copyright © 1992 Deutsche Verlags-Anstalt GmbH, Stuttgart.

This translation is published by arrangement with Deutsche
Verlags-Anstalt GmbH

English language translation Copyright © 1997 by Ingrid Taylor

This book has been produced by Aurum Press Limited,
25 Bedford Avenue, London WC1B 3AT

A catalogue record for this book is available
from the British Library.

ISBN 1 85410 473 X

10 9 8 7 6 5 4 3 2 1
2001 2000 1999 1998 1997

Typeset by Clive Dorman & Co
Printed and bound by South China Printing Co. (1988) Ltd.

Contents

Foreword and Acknowledgements

For almost twelve years we have studied the history of garden design. Our book *Italienische Gärten* was the result of many years of research in Italy. In 1985, while still preparing that work, we took a short trip to southern England, where we visited many well-known gardens. In doing so, we discovered the complex interrelations between garden design in Italy and England. We had already found in Italy that the most beautiful gardens often had either an English owner or an English designer, and now in England we found that many of the gardens revealed a very clear Italian influence in their design. In 1906, Victor Zobel, a contemporary commentator on English garden design, accurately observed: 'Garden design in England today can in a certain way be regarded as the last living descendant of Italian Renaissance gardens'[1] This statement touches on an aspect which is central to this book.

As soon as we had completed our book on Italian gardens, we turned to English garden design, taking a close look first of all at the wide variety of styles in evidence, and then concentrating on the type of garden that the English call simply a 'formal garden'.
Even on our first journey to England it was clear that in no other country in Europe can so many examples of a highly developed and lively tradition in garden design be found. Very soon we realized that we were looking at the most important works of European garden design of the 20th century.

As our emphasis is on the first few decades of the 20th century, we had at our disposal the many actual examples of gardens, and also a wealth of documentary material. We were able to refer not only to countless excellently produced folio volumes, but also to the back issues of *Country Life* and *The Studio*, journals that often feature articles on country-house gardens.

One book in particular provided us with an important point of reference. *The Formal Garden in England*, the ground-breaking work by Reginald Blomfield and Inigo Thomas, published in 1892. Today, over a hundred years later it is very interesting to take a look back at this influential document and the developments surrounding it.

We know very well that the whole area of gardens and garden design has enjoyed an enormous upsurge in popularity in recent years. Nor has it escaped our notice that countless publications, often of English origin and excellently produced, are now available everywhere. Is it possible to compete against such a flood of illustrations; has everything been said and written?

Every book we read about English gardens helped us crystallize our ideas and establish our subject more precisely. The result is neither a historical survey of gardens nor is it a practical handbook on garden design. Our main concern is to analyse the design of a particular type of garden that has changed little in its basic principles since the Middle Ages. We hope that such a systematic typological approach will, on the one hand, allow a deeper understanding of these works of art and, on the other, provide useful design guidelines for architects and garden planners. The book is also, however, a very personal appraisal of our many trips to England. If it should inspire the reader to visit these gardens, then he will also find it to be a practical source of reference in preparation.

It is in the nature of the thing that a book such as this one owes much to the help and support of many 'garden friends'. Our thanks go first to the owners of these English gardens and their representatives, all of whom, without any complicated formalities whatsoever, gave us access to their gardens and kindly took the time to answer our questions. In particular, we should like to thank

Lady Astor at Sulhamstead, Patricia Coke at Bentley, the Duke of Devonshire at Chatsworth, the Viscount De L'Isle at Penshurst, Geoffrey Howarth of the Ditchley Foundation in Chipping Norton, Lady Kleinworth in Upper Slaughter, Martin Lane Fox in Newbury, Jennie Makepeace at Parnham and Rosemary Verey at Barnsley House.

We also received exemplary support from the various British institutions we approached. For their prompt and reliable responses to all our queries, we should like to thank Isabelle van Groeningen, Emma Lindsay, Eric McBurney, Sallyann Morris and Deborah Pascoe of the National Trust in London and Cirencester. At the National Trust for Scotland, we would like to thank the Gardens; Curator, Eric Robson. Robert Elwall and Mary Nixon of the Royal Institute of British Architects (RIBA) gave us valuable help, and Patrick Ramsey and William Jackson of the Knight Frank and Rutley agency in London and Edinburgh kindly made documents available to us.

Kind thanks are also due to the many friendly gardeners whom we met, among them Pamela Schwerdt in Sissinghurst and Peter Nicholls at Hidcote.

Most of our travels in England began and ended with a stay in a house in the country surrounded by a wonderful garden – Old Cloth Hall near Cranbrook; our grateful thanks go to Katherine Morgan for her hospitality and her many garden hints.

We also thank our garden friends in Germany for their sound advice and for sharing with us their travel experiences of England. In particular, Professor Dr Ruprecht Rümler in Cologne, Gudrun and Karl-Theodor Schäfer in Karlsruhe and Dipl. Ing. Bernd Weigel in Baden-Baden. Heinrich Wenzel in Ettlingen was extremely helpful in researching botanical terms, and Phillip Woolley MA in Landau, kindly answered all our questions about English culture, geography and history. It is purely for alphabetical reasons that he stands here.

Finally, we would also like to thank Hubertus von Gemmingen for his editorial work on the German edition, Ingrid Taylor for her commanding skills as a translator, and Sheila Murphy for her commitment and conscientiousness in preparing the English edition.

Günter Mader
Laila Neubert-Mader
Ettlingen, October 1991, November 1996

*God Almighty first planted a Garden
And indeed it is the purest of Human Pleasures
It is the greatest Refreshment
to the Spirits of Man;
without which Buildings and Palaces
are but gross Handyworks
and a Man shall ever see,
that when Ages grow to Civility and Elegancy,
Man comes to Build Stately,
sooner than Garden finely:
As if Gardening were the greater Perfection.*

Francis Bacon, 1625[2]

Illustration: Charles Edward Mallows, 1910

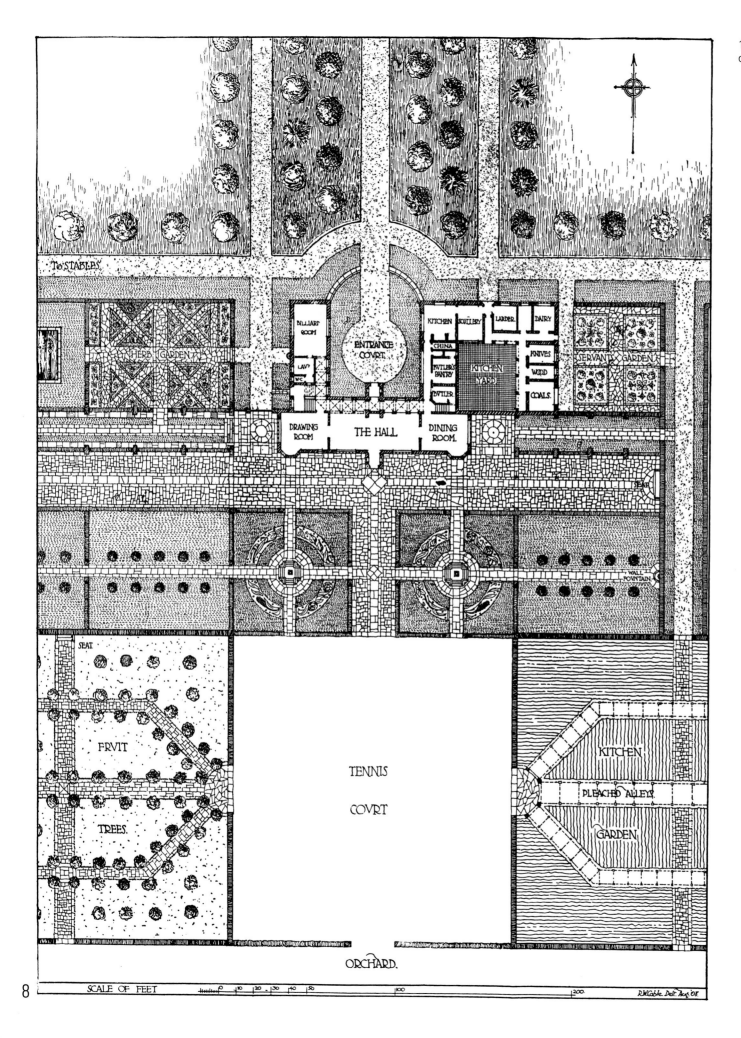

1 Ground plan of a country-house garden,
designed by Charles Edward Mallows, c.1910.

To STABLES

HERB GARDEN

BILLIARD ROOM

LAV?
WC

ENTRANCE COVRT

KITCHEN SCULLERY LARDER DAIRY

CHINA

BUTLER'S PANTRY

KITCHEN YARD

BUTLER

KNIVES WOOD COALS

SERVANTS GARDEN

DRAWING ROOM

THE HALL

DINING ROOM.

WALL FOUNTAIN

SEAT

FRUIT

TREES.

TENNIS COVRT

KITCHEN

PLEACHED ALLEY

GARDEN

ORCHARD.

SCALE OF FEET   0 10 20 30 40 50   100   200.

R.W.Gobbe. Delt. Aug '08.

Introduction

To many people, the term *English garden* is practically synonymous with *landscape garden*. The cultural influence of the English landscape garden, sometimes described as Britain's most important contribution to European art history, has been so great that it has quite unjustifiably overshadowed all other developments in garden design in England.

Even before the advent of the landscape garden, English garden design was a highly developed, skilful blend of the country's own traditions, reaching back to the Middle Ages, and to Italian, Dutch and French influences. By the middle of the 19th century, when the landscape garden style had outlived its time, people turned once again to the design ideas of the 17th century, creating out of them a new style that was to reach its peak in the first three decades of this century. Even today it is a style that still has great vigour.

This formal garden style was first conceived as a conscious antithesis to the landscape garden. Although it was a logical progression in a tradition of garden design reaching back to classical antiquity, it was initially disparaged by the defenders of the landscape garden, who saw it as a despised contrast to the one true style of garden, the supposedly *natural* landscape garden. The term *formal garden* was nevertheless adopted by the advocates of the new garden style and it soon lost its polemical undertones. A more accurate name, less laden with value judgements, might be the *architectural garden*, so described as early as 1905 by the German architect Hermann Muthesius, who was a great connoisseur of English garden design.

When asked to name the most notable garden style to emerge in Europe in the 20th century, the *English formal garden* would be our first choice. It is on a par with the landscape garden as England's chief contribution to the history of garden design. Many beautifully designed and perfectly maintained gardens in this style can still be found in Britain and this book pays due homage to them. Preceding the main part of the book is a consideration of man-made landscapes in England, as they form the basis of garden design. Gardens can be seen as focal points of landscape – a fact that is confirmed again and again in England.

The Making of the English Landscape
Geography, History, Design

Generations pass while some trees stand, and old families last not three oaks.
SIR THOMAS BROWNE[3]

Almost every stretch of the English countryside has been gradually shaped by man into a complex fabric bearing the marks of geographical, historical and economic developments. Both man and nature have always influenced the appearance of the landscape. History and culture, politics and legislation have as much power to shape the landscape as natural conditions such as topography, soil quality and climate.

   In prehistoric times Britain was mostly covered in forest and only small areas were cultivated. In the Bronze Age, around 1800 BC, the first settlements appeared and the land began to be divided up. Structures composed of animal pastures and fields emerged: near to the settlements these

a

b

c

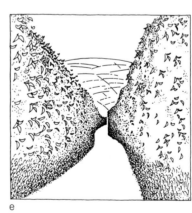

d

e

f

2   Landscapes.
a) Hedge landscape with corn fields in Somerset.
b) Typical clump of trees near Stanway in Gloucestershire.
c) Wensleydale in Yorkshire. Bare peaks and small settlements framed by trees are a typical landscape pattern in many parts of England.
d) Small areas of woodland are often surrounded by stone walls.
e) Narrow, winding country lanes, bordered by high hedges, are typical of many parts of England.
f) Trees are often found growing in hedges between fields.
g) Individual farmhouses are located mainly in hollows dotted around with trees for protection.
h) Solitary trees and edges of woodland interplay with topography to create an interesting landscape scene.
i) In many parts of England dry-stone walls take the place of hedges between fields.

3   Pasture landscape near Kirkby Malham in North Yorkshire, Yorkshire National Park. Such clumps of trees, forming in outline a single large tree, are found all over the countryside, not only in the parks.

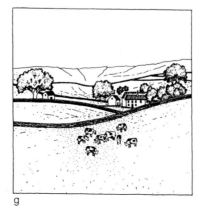

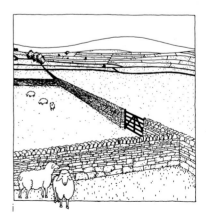

g

h

i

4 A stream with white cow-parsley in bloom, near Northwich in Cheshire.

5 Hedge landscape near Uldale in Cumbria, in the Lake District National Park.

6   Between Buckland and Stanton in Gloucestershire, the hedgebanks, or verges, are often a swathe of flowers. This picture shows white cow-parsley (*Chaerophyllum sylvestre*) in flower in May.

7   Cotswolds landscape and the village of Stanton in Gloucestershire.

enclosures were small and close together; further away the scale increased until finally they merged with the wider, as yet untouched and unclaimed countryside.

From about 1000 BC farming became increasingly intensive and many areas of woodland were cut down. This development reached a peak in Roman Britain when there was access to an enormous market for agricultural products, in particular grain and wool. The collapse of the Roman Empire meant the loss of this Continental market. As a result much farmland was left uncultivated and was eventually reclaimed by bushes and trees.

In the Middle Ages, following centuries of stagnation, the old landscape structures gradually began to fill again with new life. Massive changes to the landscape occurred in the 12th and 13th centuries as more and more arable land was required for the needs of a growing population. In large areas of the countryside woods were again cut down and heath and moorland reclaimed.

In the middle of the 14th century all these developments came to a standstill when half the population fell victim to the plague. The demand for agricultural produce dropped sharply and there was a general shortage of labour to work the fields. In many cases farmers switched to sheep farming, which was less labour-intensive than tilling the fields.

During the 15th century the wool trade flourished. Large numbers of sheep were now being kept all over the country and land-owners looked for ways to extend their available grazing land. One way in which they did this was to take over abandoned tracts of land, but in the 16th century this practice met with strong opposition, especially when the great land-owners also enclosed common land, thus depriving smallholders and tenant farmers of an important part of their livelihood. Large numbers of people began to leave the countryside and move to the towns where manufacturing was beginning to offer impoverished country people an alternative means of earning a living. The process of urbanization intensified, leading to an increased demand for foodstuffs, a demand that could only be satisfied through efficient agricultural production. Consumption of building material and fuel also rose, bringing with it in the 16th and 17th centuries devastating consequences for the woods and forests.[4]

One of the first to recognize the tragedy in this development was the scholar John Evelyn. In 1664 he published a work entitled *Sylva (or a Discourse of Forest Trees)*,[5] dedicated to the king, in which he appealed to the large land-owners, urging them to appreciate the diversity and beauty of the trees, and to recognize the economic necessity of active reafforestation. Evelyn expressed his concern, too, that dwindling stocks of trees would have serious consequences for England's shipbuilding industry, which was of great political and economic significance to the country. Clearly his work was the expression of a new spirit. Such was the popularity of his book that it was reprinted many times, and the great English passion for trees developed, a passion evident to the present day. Tree-planting became a virtuous practice throughout the land. In countless 17th- and 18th-century paintings and etchings of country houses the artists have taken considerable pains to show planted rows of trees, avenues and woods.

In the 18th and 19th centuries a widespread restructuring of agriculture became necessary. The ever-increasing process of urbanization and the beginnings of industrialization led to a sharp rise in the need for agricultural produce. Output was increased by streamlining land utilization. Depending on soil quality in a particular area, agriculture was concentrated on either grain production, sheep-rearing or dairy cattle. The countryside became divided up into distinct 'corn counties' and 'grazing counties'. Current statistics put the number of sheep in the British Isles at about 43 million,[6] and to visitors from the Continent the sheep pastures are one of the most noticeable features of the English countryside. The familiar central and southern European picture of the shepherd and his dog watching over a flock of sheep is contrasted in England with grazing flocks dispersed across wide expanses of land.

Between 1760 and 1860 Parliament introduced a series of Enclosure Acts, which resulted in a complete reorganization of almost half the land in England. All local district councils had to prepare plans showing how the land was divided and put forward approval proposals for reallocation. New tracts of land were reclaimed, smaller fields were joined together, new roads built and rivers straightened. The Enclosure Acts stipulated that the new divisions should be marked out by hedges and that all fields and pastures had to be enclosed. Within the space of a century some 320,000 kilometres (200,000 miles) of hedges were planted in line with this scheme.[7] Throughout the country nurseries sprang up to provide the requisite number of trees and plants.

The most interesting source on the history of man-made landscapes in England is *Britannia Illustrata*, published in 1707 by the illustrator Leonard Knyff and the copper engraver Jan Kip.[8] Containing 80 bird's-eye views of country houses, it not only documents precisely how the houses and gardens looked but is also very informative about the surrounding landscape. Even a cursory glance at this collection of engravings will reveal many arrow-straight, tree-lined avenues disappearing off towards the horizon in practically all the illustrations. Such avenues were a very distinctive feature of landscapes in the 17th and 18th centuries. The engravings also show how rows of trees marked out fields and the courses of rivers and streams. There is very little evidence of larger forests, only occasional patches of more open woodland, orchards or small plantations hardly bigger than a field. Nevertheless, these areas would still have provided the necessary habitat for game. The illustrators seem to have considered it important to depict magnificent herds of red deer standing in front of these woods, probably to underline the link between forest and game, and to emphasize the gentry's privileges in terms of game preservation and hunting.

The main features of a landscape, as depicted in Kip's engravings, can for the most part still be seen in today's countryside. In particular, two types of landscape are found: the park landscape and the hedge landscape. Generally, one or the other of these types dominates, but sometimes the two are seen in combination.

Typical of a park landscape is a loose structure of meadows, fields, small woods, tree-lined avenues, rows and groups of trees and some splendid specimen trees. The stands of trees may often be quite dense, but they seldom merge into continuous woodland. Nowhere else in Europe are such magnificent trees to be seen as in England. Particularly impressive are the oaks, chestnuts, limes, ash and beech. But anyone with an eye for the beauty of the wonderful mature specimens cannot fail also to notice the many diseased trees among them and the devastation caused in recent years by storms. Wind-damaged trees, dead branches and leafless skeletons were, however, not uncommon in the landscapes of previous

centuries, as evidenced by old landscape paintings. It seems such shapes were even thought to be rather picturesque. Today, as in the days of John Evelyn, the most effective remedy for the painful loss of trees is to plant new ones.

The most characteristic landscape in Britain is without doubt the hedge landscape. In most areas of the countryside, from Kent to Scotland and from Cornwall to Norfolk, one can find a mosaic-like pattern of pastures and fields enclosed in hedges. They cast a seemingly endless net across the wide expanse of the countryside. Even the winding country lanes and paths are bordered with hedges, only allowing glimpses of the surrounding countryside at the tops of hills or through gateways to fields. Despite the expanse of landscape the overwhelming impression is one of a sequence of smaller spaces.

The plant most commonly found in hedges is the hawthorn. In thicker hedges this is mixed with hazel, hornbeam, privet, elder, wild cherry, rowan, crab apple and pussy willow. Intertwined with these are brambles, dog rose and ivy. The range of plants in a hedge is a good indicator of its age. As a rule of thumb, the number of different varieties of bush found in a hedge 30 metres long is equivalent to the age of the hedge in centuries. A hedge planted in Victorian times generally only has one variety, whereas a hedge from Tudor times will have five or six. The line and width of a hedge are also indicators of age. Straight, narrow hedges are mostly 18th or 19th century in origin, but wider hedges following the natural lie of the land are often several hundred years old, some even dating back to early medieval times. Every one to two years the hedges between the fields are cut back by the farmers.

In the course of the 1960s and 1970s the advent of new, bigger machinery brought with it

a need to create larger and larger fields; many hedges disappeared as a result of these changes to field patterns. Fortunately, this trend has been slowed as a result of the increased environmental awareness that emerged in the 1980s, and through the introduction of new laws to protect the countryside.

Often hedges are planted at irregular intervals with large trees, mostly oak, ash or elm, occasionally lime and beech (see Fig. 5). A 17th-century publication encouraged land-owners to plant fruit trees here and there in the hedges, to provide wayfarers and workers in the fields with welcome and free refreshment.[9] Mixing hedges and trees was common practice even in the Middle Ages, when the reasons were primarily to do with efficiency and economy. Trees in a hedge were not in the farmer's way and they did not take up as much room as a patch of land given over to forest. Even at the time of the Enclosure Acts trees were often planted in hedges.

A rich variety of wild flowers grew alongside the bushes and trees in hedges, and a very pretty sight are the verges, strips of ground, sometimes several metres wide, between the hedge and the road; in April these are studded with sulphur-yellow primroses (*Primula auricula*), or the rich hue of bluebells in May with white cow-parsley (*Chaerophyllum sylvestre*, see Fig. 6) and in summer with blue meadow crane's bill (*Geranium pratense*). These flowers do, of course, occur in combination with others throughout the year, but at any one time or place, one variety will provide the dominant colour. Perhaps these strips of flower-meadow with their subtle colour tones were a source of inspiration for the excellent designs for flower borders found in English gardens (see pp. 98ff.).

It is not the purpose of this book to analyse the 15

ecology of a hedge, but one aspect that must be mentioned is that hedges offer a habitat for a great variety of wildlife. They are a home to birds, insects, mice and moles, stoats and weasels and hedgehogs.

In many areas, especially in the Yorkshire Dales, the Peak District, the Lake District and the Cotswolds, hedges around fields are replaced by dry-stone walls. Such walls have a tradition that goes back thousands of years, and they can be regarded as a remnant of prehistoric times. In many ways these walls are very similar to those found in typical old agricultural regions around the Mediterranean. This is both an indication of a shared heritage from an ancient megalithic culture, but also of the many links between the regions during the period of Roman rule. Walls were generally used instead of hedges in places where the topsoil was too poor to support a hedge. They were also useful as a convenient place to put the many stones removed from the cultivated fields. Even today these old walls perform a function in terms of enclosing grazing land and they are therefore regularly maintained almost everywhere. The most impressive landscape with fields bordered by dry-stone walls is seen today in the heart of Yorkshire, in the Yorkshire Dales.

Many of the different types of landscape encountered in Britain today have a very pleasing and harmonious design. In his book on the perception of landscape, the English geographer Jay Appleton took a psychological approach in his analysis of human perceptions of the components of a landscape. He established two central and basic human requirements – of refuge and of prospect, in other words the need for protection and the need for a view.[10] Hedges and trees are therefore perceived as providing the necessary protective elements, yet a view into the distance is also very appealing. Where a landscape fulfils both of these requirements, that is where people will feel most at home.

The History of English Garden Design

Garden Design in the Middle Ages and in the Renaissance

Although no actual examples of gardens designed in the Middle Ages and the Renaissance are still in existence, we can still obtain a very good impression of what they were like from old manuscripts, woodcuts, engravings and book illustrations. Gardens first began to appear at the end of the 15th century – political confusion had prevented any notable progress before that time. Then, under the reign of Queen Elizabeth I (r. 1558–1603), garden design began to make great strides. England now had links with the developments taking place in Italy that were giving rise to a new culture throughout Europe. Elizabeth encouraged the landed gentry to lavish more attention on their country homes and as a result of her many travels throughout England she prompted them to create suitably representative estates. One of the most remarkable gardens of that time was at Kenilworth, the home of Lord Leicester, and another was Theobalds, the country seat of Lord Burleigh, both of which were created around 1575. England, too, now had its artistically designed gardens.

It is easy to trace this development through the many documents and writings of the time. At first, contemporary literature concentrated on practical advice for the gardener, giving information on, for example, sowing, care of seedlings, fertilizing, watering, pruning and grafting trees, and on sweet-smelling herbs and flowers. The earliest literary sources on the history of English garden design are the writings of Thomas Hill, which were published under various titles between 1563 and 1608, but which in the main have the same contents. The most comprehensive edition of his

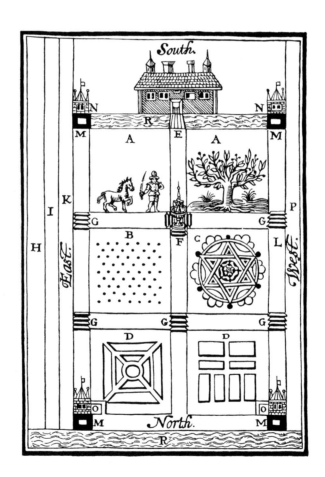

9 Woodcut from *A New Orchard and Garden* by William Lawson, published in 1618.

work is *The Gardener's Labyrinth*, published in 1571 under the pseudonym Dydymus Mountain, and attractively illustrated with many beautiful woodcuts. Its objective is primarily to describe garden practice, but it also gives an idea of the types of garden design. Generally speaking, gardens in the 16th century were always enclosed within high walls (walled gardens) or hedges (enclosed gardens), as in the Middle Ages. A key element of Italian Renaissance gardens – the incorporation into the design of a view of the surrounding countryside – was adopted only much later in English gardens.

Walls and hedges not only closed off the garden from the outside, but were also used within the garden itself to section off the different functional zones. Areas of practical benefit and areas for pure decoration were placed side-by-side to form an overall structure. At first the arrangement was purely incremental. There was no artistic interpretation of spatial sequences nor any attempt to integrate the house into the design, such as was evident in the Italian Renaissance style. The English garden of the 16th century was thus still very firmly rooted in the medieval model. In contrast to Italian custom, the areas of the garden for practical use, i.e. the orchard and the kitchen garden, were the most important parts. Generally, the kitchen garden also included a rectangular fishpond in which fish were bred for the table.

Increasingly, however, during the course of the 16th century, sections of the garden were developed into pleasure gardens. Gradually England, too, like France, Germany and Holland, was beginning to feel the Italian influence, through both direct and indirect channels. This was a key step in the development of garden design. Artists and craftsmen from Italy were engaged at court.

Noblemen, merchants and scholars travelled to all parts of Italy and saw there the latest designs in architecture and gardens. Copper engravings and *vedutas* depicting Italian gardens were soon common in all the royal courts in Europe and were used as models.

The pleasure gardens arising in the 16th century consisted on the one hand of flower gardens with tulips, violets, primulas, daffodils, veronica, marigolds, roses and Madonna lilies and, on the other, of herb gardens with medicinal, sweet-smelling and culinary herbs such as thyme, sage, rosemary, lavender, marjoram, mint and hyssop. Generally, pleasure gardens also had a maze. It can be assumed that the idea for such mazes came from Italy. In the very well-known engraving of the Villa d'Este by Etienne Du Pérac in 1573, several mazes can be seen in the bottom part of the gardens.[11] This engraving, of which there were many copies at the time, may well have been an inspiration. Particularly characteristic of 16th-century English garden design were knot gardens, or sections laid out in complicated patterns of box or herbs. This form, too, was probably based on Italian ideas. In the *Hypnerotomachia Poliphili* there is also a woodcut showing a knot garden.[12]

Another typical element was topiary work, which consisted of bushes (box, cypress or juniper) clipped into shapes. Stone obelisks, fountains, pergolas, sculptures and small garden pavilions were also a feature of all country house gardens by the end of the 16th century, in England as elsewhere. All these elements came indisputably from Italian garden design, directly and indirectly.

One specifically English aspect, which has no equivalent in Italy, seems to have been the great preference for bowling greens. By 1540

10 This woodcut from *The Gardener's Labyrinth* by Thomas Hill, published in 1571, shows a small parterre garden surrounded by a fence.

11 A remarkable detail in this woodcut from *The Gardener's Labyrinth* is the marking string seen in the top left-hand corner. This is a very old technique in laying out a garden, i.e. imposing a geometric order and thus declaring man's mastery over a plot of land.

a lawn on which to play bowls was already a well-established part of every larger-sized garden.

Finally, an important component of English country-house gardens was the mount, an artificial hill from which one could view the garden. This also seems to have been a uniquely English contribution to garden design. Perhaps its aim was to provide the kind of vistas enjoyed in Italian gardens. Or possibly it was some re-interpretation of archaic Celtic burial mounds, or maybe simply a way of satisfying people's quite natural desire to have a view. The best impression we can gain today of what these mounts were like is at Packwood House in Warwickshire. Here a path edged with tidily clipped box hedges spirals up to a viewing point at the top of the 6-metre (20-ft) high mount. Such features may indeed be highly original and have a certain playful charm, but they lack a more refined integration into the general picture. As can be seen from old engravings, the mount was almost always a singular, non-integrated form in the overall garden design.

Garden Design in the Seventeenth Century

Books, paintings and engravings are also the main source material for information on garden design in the 17th century. *The Country Farm* by Gervase Markham was published in 1615. This collection of practical tips and hints for orchards, kitchen gardens and herb gardens contains many small woodcut illustrations and is strongly influenced by French garden literature. The same author wrote another gardening book, *A Way to get Wealth*, published in 1630. By 1695 15 editions had appeared, and we can assume that it had a great influence on garden design in the 17th century. A contemporary and friend of Markham was William Lawson, whose two garden books were also very successful. In 1617 Lawson published *The Country Housewife's Garden* and in 1618, *A New Orchard and Garden*.

One of the most important and well-known documents on English garden design in the 17th century is the essay 'Of Gardens', published in 1625 by the statesman and essayist, Francis Bacon. In the centuries since it first appeared this description of a garden has been taken again and again as a reference point by garden theorists and garden designers. Although Bacon would most certainly have known many Elizabethan country-house gardens, his text gives practically no definite information on the structure of these gardens. His essay owes more to the genre of literary descriptions of gardens, in the style of *Roman de la Rose* by Guillaume de Lorris or in the spirit of Francesco Colonna's *Hypnerotomachia Poliphili*. Nevertheless, Bacon's essay does confirm the importance of gardens in the 17th century.

In comparison to Francesco Colonna's description of a garden written almost 150 years previously, it is noticeable that Bacon makes no mythological reference, and that his passion for gardens has a very practical bias. It seems as if Bacon had direct knowledge of the many plants he described, and that he had a great love of them. For Bacon, too, the garden is a formal structure. The elements that had been developed in the 16th century – tree-lined alleys, pergolas, hedges, topiary, pavilions, ponds, lawns and mounts – were all by now firmly established in the iconography of garden design. One aspect that is a little surprising to us is the idea of integrating a 'heath' into the design as a piece of 'natural wildness' in

juxtaposition with the formal parts of the garden. This can also be seen in the gardens of the late Renaissance in Italy. Here the *bosco* was in contrast to the strictly geometrically laid-out parts of the garden. The attempt to bring 'natural wildness' into the garden runs like a leitmotif through the history of English garden design. Examples from the 20th century are particularly well conceived.

As previously mentioned, one of the most impressive documents in the history of English garden design is *Britannia Illustrata*, a collection of 80 engravings showing bird's-eye views of English country houses. The work was published in 1707, but the illustrations originate from towards the end of the 17th century. They were drawn over a period of eight years by Leonard Knyff and then engraved in copper by Jan Kip, in two years. This work was modelled on similar collections of engravings produced on the Continent, for example the French work by Jacques Androuet du Cerceau, published in 1568 and entitled *Les Plus Excellents Bastiments de France*.

Britannia Illustrata contains illustrations of country houses and gardens dating mostly from the second half of the 17th century. These large-scale, artistically designed estates were by no means inferior to the princely residences on the Continent. All of the gardens are of course formal gardens. As in the Italian Renaissance villas, the house and garden have grown into a single conceptual unit, with rows of trees and tree-lined avenues radiating out in all directions, linking the estate with the surrounding countryside.

None of the gardens illustrated in *Britannia Illustrata* has survived. However, one or two of the houses are still in existence, and they prove that the engravings were indeed very accurately drawn. Towards the end of the 19th century these

engravings were an important source of information for the revival of the formal garden. All garden designers drew upon the book, which provided English examples and traditions to inspire them. Even now, *Britannia Illustrata* is a source of inspiration to designers. In some instances certain sections of these gardens have been reconstructed using the information contained in the engravings.

Garden Design in the Eighteenth Century

At the beginning of the 18th century a style of garden developed that had little in common with the forms of garden design known up to that point. This new style was not drawn from the traditions of practical garden design, but derived from literary images. The first ideas in this direction came from Joseph Addison (1672–1719), in his *Essays*, published in 1710, in which he described landscapes dotted with charming little Arcadian temples. These images exactly fitted in with newly emerging, naturalist attitudes in the 18th century. Soon, such literary visions were to become real designs.

Alexander Pope (1688–1714) was the first to take this step. On his estate in Twickenham he created the first freely designed garden. Although a few familiar elements, such as a mount, a bowling green, a grotto and a garden temple, did in fact appear in the design, these were not incorporated into any fixed plan, but were placed freely in the landscape. Pope was contemptuous of the formal gardens of earlier times, condemned any intervention in nature and demanded that his garden

12 This engraving appeared in *Britannia Illustrata*, published in 1707. It shows the garden of Grimsthorpe Castle in Lincolnshire, which has the typical features of a garden of the 17th and 18th centuries: tree-lined alleys, rows of trees, orchards, parterres, pavilions, a kitchen garden, a pergola and a bowling green. The house and part of the gardens are still in existence.

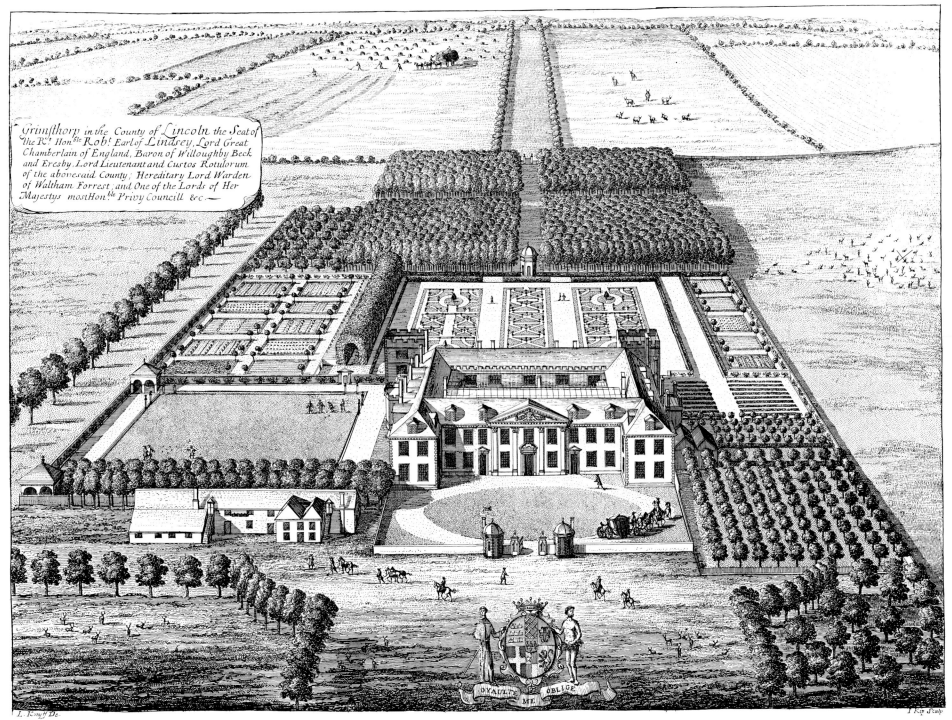

designers produce a sensitive imitation of nature. He categorically rejected clipped hedges, straight lines and right angles. Man's design activities should not make a garden into a formal structure, but turn it into a narrative or a painting. Garden design was understood as a blending of nature, poetry and painting. William Kent (1685–1748) produced designs fully in accord with this ideal. Lancelot Brown (1716–83), nicknamed Capability Brown by virtue of his skill, was William Kent's successor. He completed the landscape garden at Stowe in Buckinghamshire, which had been conceived and designed by Kent, and in 1763 he designed the garden at Blenheim in Oxfordshire. Brown followed the same style as his predecessor, but used water in a completely new way as a design element. He dammed streams to create lakes with curving shorelines. Water was directed down cascades and Palladian-style bridges spanned the river at narrow points. Under George III Capability Brown was appointed Royal Gardener. A new style of garden was now firmly established and more and more examples of the work of Brown and his staff sprang up around the country.

Around 1750 the first reports of Chinese gardens reached Europe. Their design was also based on artistic and not formal principles, and this was taken as confirmation that a garden can be viewed as an idealized landscape. In 1757 William Chambers (1723–96) wrote a book documenting his impressions of Chinese garden design, formed on a journey in that country. The same year he was commissioned to design Kew Gardens, and included a Chinese pagoda as an attraction. Since then small exotic buildings have been an essential component of the landscape garden.

Through constant copying and many unsuitable additions the landscape garden style entered a period of crisis at the end of the 18th century. One problem lay in the fact that, increasingly, ever-smaller spaces were being landscaped. At this point the style began to attract quite justified criticism. Hermann Muthesius wrote of this time, 'The time of natural motifs is now past. ... So-called landscape design, with its winding paths and artificial streams, subsided into a virtual parady of garden design when applied to small gardens. There was a period when people were tired of order and believed that progress lay in avoiding order and replacing it instead with the irregularities of natural forms. The landscape garden has dominated garden design for almost a hundred years and only very recently has it been finally overcome.'[13] However, no criticism of the landscape garden should omit to mention that it, too, was a style basically concerned with sculptural and spatial design, and one that tried to achieve a particular artistic effect using land, water, lawns, trees and bushes. Although no geometrically structured plan lies behind the landscape garden, it is also based on spatial division, sight lines, rhythm, planes, volumes and colour.

Garden Design in the Nineteenth Century

At the beginning of the 19th century the ideals of Capability Brown lost ground. Humphrey Repton (1752–1818) was one of the first to look for new directions. Terraces, balustrades and gardens steps, all elements from the model gardens of the Italian Renaissance, were reintroduced, but in a monumentally exaggerated form that today we find unattractive. The landscape garden was now used only as a background. New varieties of trees and bushes were introduced from abroad and this took away the compositional tautness of the landscape garden, making it rather colourful and full of strong contrasts. At the same time these trees imported from all corners of the globe were an ever-present symbol of the extent and power of the British Empire.

Flowers, which had played no part in the landscape garden, found a place again in garden design. Popular uses were in ornate rosariums, small rose gardens and regularly laid out flower beds. Atmospheric rock gardens, or gardens with subtropical plants also enjoyed great popularity.

In the middle of the 19th century interest was reawakened in a type of garden whose forms were more closely related to the gardens of the 17th century than to the florid designs of the Victorian age. The garden was again seen as a sequence of individual spaces separated from each other by walls or hedges. The outer limits were once more clearly defined. A more human scale was reintroduced, one familiar from the early Italian Renaissance gardens. Penshurst Place in Kent and Arley Hall in Cheshire, both created around 1860 and still excellently maintained, can be regarded as the most notable forerunners of this new understanding of garden design.

An outstanding figure in garden design in the 19th century was William Robinson (1838–1935), who made a name for himself as a gardener, plant collector and writer. Of his many publications, the most influential were *The Wild Garden* (1870) and *The English Flower Garden* (1883), which established him as one of the most important forerunners of 20th-century garden design. Robinson made a complete break with the forms of garden design prevalent in his time, rejecting in particular the bedding schemes planted with colourful

13 Country house in Denbighshire in Wales. This painting, by an unknown artist, dates from 1662 and is now in the collections of Yale University in New Haven (original size of section, approx. 75 x 100 cm (29 x 39 in). The walled gardens, beautiful gateways, water games and flights of steps all reveal the clear influence of Italian ideas in garden design.

14 This work, painted in 1680 by an unknown Dutch master and also in the collections of Yale University, shows the garden of Pierrepoint House in Nottinghamshire (original size of painting, 91 x 122 cm (36 x 48 in). It shows a sunken garden that is a special design feature described in detail on pages 92–7.

annuals; here plants served simply to create a particular colour effect; no attempt was made to make people aware of the beauty of flowers themselves. Robinson saw himself primarily as a flower gardener. Unlike his predecessors, he appreciated the rich variety in nature and sought to exploit this design potential in his gardens. Always aware of the relationship between plants and their surroundings, he discovered the beauty of wood anemones dotted among trees by a meadow, of foxglove growing in a clearing, of ivy and other twining plants climbing around a tree trunk. It is true that Romantic painters had also discovered these charms, but it was Robinson who made such beauties acceptable in gardens. As a gardener he made use of much that had been gathered by plant collectors a generation before. He believed that planting a garden was like painting a picture. The finished garden should have a picturesque quality; it should induce one to paint.

Although William Robinson proved to be an important early influence on garden design in the 20th century, he was firmly against the formal garden. He became a bitter opponent of Reginald Blomfield (1856–1942) and Inigo Thomas (1866–1950), whose work, *The Formal Garden in England*, laid down the most important theoretical basis for the formal garden in the 20th century. The book was published in 1892 and immediately aroused great interest. A second edition appeared that same year. Blomfield and Thomas were architects and thus garden design and not horticulture was the declared aim of their treatise. They were as much against Robinson's naturalism as they were against the thoughtless flower-bed arrangements in the Victorian style. They regarded the garden as a logical extension of the house and as a structure composed of individual spaces with different functions. The definition of the formal garden is reproduced opposite.

Garden Design in the Twentieth Century

If William Robinson and Reginald Blomfield can be regarded as the two central figures in garden design in the late 19th century, then that role is assumed at the start of the 20th century by Gertrude Jekyll (1843–1932) and Sir Edwin Lutyens (1869–1944). What to Robinson and Blomfield were incompatible opposites were combined by Jekyll and Lutyens into a single, harmonious whole. Gertrude Jekyll's approach was in the same vein as Robinson's, and Edwin Lutyens, an architect, was of a similar school to that of Blomfield and Thomas.

It was in 1889 that a fortunate circumstance first brought Lutyens, who was at the time just 20, together with the 45-year-old artist, Gertrude Jekyll; this meeting was to mark the beginning of a partnership that was to last for decades and through more than one hundred joint projects for garden designs. Gertrude Jekyll had trained as a painter and she was familiar with a wide range of craft techniques. Since 1868 she had been a garden designer and had photographed and written about garden subjects in many newspaper articles and books. She herself had a large garden and was a passionate collector of plants. As a gardener she had a great deal of practical experience, but no professional training; she described herself as a working amateur. It was her finely tuned planting schemes that won her greatest attention. She looked not only for good colour combinations, but sought to enhance the colour effect by intermingling flowers with suitable foliage plants. 'My main aim is always to create a beautiful picture',[14] she stated, revealing clearly that she designed as a painter. The significance and success of Gertrude Jekyll's work lay in just this approach. She brought the experience and visual understanding of the painter to garden design, but – it is important to recognize – without calling into question the overall articulation and shape of the garden as determined by the architect. On the contrary, she used the strict order and regulation of the garden as an ideal frame for her pictures.

Edwin Lutyens, who was discovered and encouraged in his career by Gertrude Jekyll, built two large country houses when he was only 21. One of them was Munstead Wood near Godalming in Surrey, commissioned by his patron, Jekyll. Through Jekyll and later also his wife, Lady Emily Lytton, Edwin Lutyens gained entry into the very best social circles, which led him into many new commissions to build or redesign country houses and their associated gardens. In 1900, to have a 'Lutyens house' and a 'Jekyll garden' was the very epitome of a fine lifestyle. Lutyens designed the building, and also the overall and detailed arrangement of space in the garden; Jekyll designed the planting scheme and controlled the final look. As confirmed by the architecture critic, Lawrence Weaver, in 1925,[15] her experience and sensitivities as an artist and connoisseur of European garden design meant that she had a highly developed sense of style and an understanding of overall artistic effect. She was thus an ideal influence on the young and very talented Lutyens.

A key position in the history of 20th-century garden design is occupied by Hidcote Manor in Gloucestershire (see pp. 174ff.). This garden was laid out between 1907 and 1914 by Lawrence Johnston, and, although it did not immediately meet with the kind of acclaim enjoyed by the gardens of Lutyens and Jekyll, it can be seen, in retrospect, to have been extremely influential. In Hidcote, too, the ideals of Robinson and Blomfield were convincingly brought together into a harmonious whole. In contrast to Lutyens's work, however, the formal style is less evident at Hidcote; it has a looser spatial arrangement and integrates several naturalistically designed sections into the overall picture.

The 1930s and the immediate post-war period were characterized by two completely opposing trends. On the one side were the traditionalists, holding faith with the guidelines laid down by Edwin Lutyens and Gertrude Jekyll, and on the other were designers who sought to put into practice the ideas of the modern movement, which had been developing in art and architecture on the Continent since the 1920s. The liberal, playful treatment of form and colour, such as taught by Paul Klee and Wassily Kandinsky at the Bauhaus, were a challenge to garden designers. The idea that balance was not only to be found in geometry, regularity and axiality, but also in free art and free composition, drew strength from the newly discovered and admired Japanese style of garden design. The most notable designer working in this modern style in the 1930s was Christopher Tunnard. Contemporary photographs and perspective drawings of his work give us a very good idea of the sensational effect his gardens must have had at the time, although today they seem quite dull. The smooth white walls, the concrete paving slabs and the arbitrary curves of walls, hedges and paths – all of this we now regard as somewhat undisciplined, and it no longer impresses us. The expanses of unbroken colour from much-lauded new varieties also appear to us to be excessively loud, the beds seem too colourful and a far cry from the sensitive treatment of colour and plant form, as taught by Gertrude Jekyll.

The most important contributor to garden design in the 1930s and in the post-war period

Reginald Blomfield, Inigo Thomas:
The Formal Garden in England

The question at issue is a very simple one. Is the garden to be considered in relation to the house, and as an integral part of a design which depends for its success on the combined effect of house and garden; or is the house to be ignored in dealing with the garden? ... The formal treatment of gardens ought, perhaps, to be called the architectural treatment of gardens, for it consists in the extension of the principles of design which govern the house to the grounds which surround it. ... The object of formal gardening is to bring the two into harmony, to make the house grow out of its surroundings, and to prevent its being an excrescence on the face of nature. The building cannot resemble anything in nature, unless you are content with a mud hut and cover it with grass. Architecture in any shape has certain definite characteristics which it cannot get rid of; but, on the other hand, you can lay out the grounds, and alter the levels, and plant hedges and trees exactly as you please; in a word, you can so control and modify the grounds as to bring nature into harmony with the house, if you cannot bring the house into harmony with nature. The harmony arrived at is not any trick of imitation, but an affair of a dominant idea which stamps its impress on house and grounds alike. ... A house, or any other building, ... is regular, it presents straight lines and geometrical curves. Any but the most ill-considered efforts in building – anything with any title to the name of architecture – implies premeditated form in accordance with certain limits and necessities. However picturesque the result, however bravely some chimney breaks the sky-line, or some gable contradicts another, all architecture implies restraint, and if not symmetry, at least balance. There is order everywhere and there is no escaping it. Now, suppose this visible object dropped, let us say from heaven, into the middle of a piece of ground, and this piece of ground laid out with a studied avoidance of all order, all balance, all definite lines, and the result must be a hopeless disagreement between the house and its surroundings. This very effect can be seen in the efforts of the landscape gardener, and in old country houses ... . There is a gaunt, famished, incomplete look about these houses, which is due quite as much to the felt want of relation between the house and its grounds, as to any associations of decay.[16]

25

15 Longleat House near Warminster in Wiltshire. This splendid country house is set in a landscape garden designed in the 18th century by 'Capability' Brown. The garden areas close to the house were redesigned as a formal garden in the 1930s by Russell Page.

was the writer Vita Sackville-West (1892–1962). She knew Edwin Lutyens and Gertrude Jekyll personally and her designs were a very convincing continuation of their style. Between 1930 and 1938 she and her husband, the diplomat and journalist, Harold Nicolson, created the garden at Sissinghurst Castle in Kent (see pp. 194ff.), which is quite rightly regarded as one of the most important English gardens this century. From 1946 Vita Sackville-West wrote a highly respected column on gardening in the *Observer*, and, in the period after World War II, she became the leading figure in garden design, her own garden being a mecca for garden designers throughout the world, which still remains the case today.

Another important influence on garden design in the 1930s and in the post-war period was the design work of Sir Geoffrey Jellicoe (1900–96). He trained as an architect and set up his own practice when he was 27. In 1925 he published his first book, a work that was to have a great influence on garden designers in the 20th century. This slim volume, which he wrote with John Shepherd, was called *Italian Gardens of the Renaissance*. Although concise, this summary of Italian garden design is illustrated with many drawings that gave a much deeper insight into Italian Renaissance gardens than any previously published works. In the opinion of the garden historian Jane Brown, the book caused a greater stir among garden

designers in the 1920s and 1930s than any other work, and in its wake Italian ideas once again came to influence English garden design.

In the 1930s Geoffrey Jellicoe was able to put his theories into practice in a number of gardens. Important early commissions were the redesign and extension of the gardens at Ditchley Park and Pusey House, both in Oxfordshire, and at Mottisfont Abbey in Hampshire (see Figs. 20, 27, 109). These gardens, which are still in existence today, show Jellicoe's mastery of his craft, and enable us to see quite clearly the influence of Italian garden design. Sutton Place in Surrey is the largest and most important of Jellicoe's gardens. He was commissioned to design it in 1980 when he was 80 years old. It is modern, but it is also a formal garden with all the characteristics and elements described in this book as typical of the type. Its modernity is not only expressed by the incorporation of modern sculptures (by Ben Nicholson, Henry Moore and Joan Miró), but also through the modern adaptations of details such as paving, pergolas, portals, trellises for climbing plants and fountains. However, this modernity leads to a certain detachment in the design that is not entirely to be welcomed. Perhaps the somewhat impersonal impression arises because Sutton Place was not finished, and Jellicoe did not have the support of a keenly interested owner's support. Stanley Seeger, the oil magnate who

commissioned Jellicoe, proved to be an ideal client, but just a few years later he suddenly decided to sell the property.

One of Jellicoe's most distinguished designer-colleagues was Russell Page (1906–86), who worked in partnership with Jellicoe from 1928 until the beginning of the war. After the war Page lived for many years in France. There, and in Italy, Switzerland and many other countries, he created many excellent gardens, always with a leaning towards the formal garden. His most famous project carried out in England was the redesign of the gardens of Longleat in Wiltshire (see Fig. 15).

A look at the current situation in English garden design leads one to conclude that the modern language evident in Sutton Place has remained without a successor.

Today there are essentially two main spheres of activity in English garden design: the many gardens of the National Trust, and the larger gardens in private ownership. In both cases the gardens are either kept in the original style or are reconstructions of traditional styles. The designs always have a strong restorative spirit and the ideas behind them differ little from those set out at the beginning of the century. Some may see in this a lack of creativity in garden design, but for us it is proof that many of the principles expounded here are timeless. The main aim of this present volume is to discuss these design principles.

The Formal Garden in the Twentieth Century

The Origins of the Formal Garden

In 1897, the year of Queen Victoria's sixtieth Jubilee, the British Empire spanned the globe and was at its peak. The ever-increasing wealth of Victorian England was based on the one hand on the colonies and Britain's worldwide trade links, and on the other on the Industrial Revolution, which brought with it levels of productivity much higher than ever before. England was also the first country in Europe to suffer the unbelievable devastation that accompanied industrialization. Social misery among the working class, a drastic drop in living standards in the cities and the cultural decline of utility goods – this was the price of industrialization. Dissatisfaction with the situation therefore soon grew, along with the Romantic transfiguration of the past. Industrialization could not be stopped, but important new ideas of far-reaching influence did begin to develop. John Ruskin (1819–1900) and William Morris (1834–96), both artists and social reformers, were the first embittered opponents of the new machine age and forerunners of a more general opposition. Their main criticism was of the lack of taste displayed in industrially manufactured products and of the superficial historicising and eclecticism in architecture. Ruskin and Morris pleaded for the revival of craft based on art, as well as for a vernacular, more traditional style of architecture. Reserve, simplicity and sound craft principles were the design criteria intended to combat short-lived, industrial products manufactured without regard to aesthetic values.

Around 1880, these views led to the formation of what is today generally known as the Arts and Crafts movement. It can be regarded as one of the most important and influential developments in English art history. In the 1880s a whole range of different artists' – and architects' – associations started up, based on the Arts and Crafts princples.

Among their adherents were some of the most important architects in Britain: for example, Charles Ashbee, Richard Lethaby, Edwin Lutyens, Charles Mallows, Thomas Mawson, Harold Peto, Edward Prior, Baillie Scott, Richard Shaw, Charles Voysey and Philip Webb. They all shared romantic ideals about design, views that did in fact lead to a new stylistic direction. As Gavin Stamp wrote in *The English House 1860–1914*, 'Nostalgia can be a very creative force'.[17] Today the word nostalgia is often associated with superficial imitation. Yet, as the works of Philip Webb and his contemporaries show, the concept of nostalgia, as understood by the artists of the Arts and Crafts movement, meant a reflection on, and recollection of, tried and trusted values and national and regional characteristics. This new approach broke the dominance of the classical style, and enabled a rediscovery of the rich variety of design in the many examples of medieval secular architecture still in existence. Now, for the first time, people began to take a fresh look at old farmhouses and cottages and to appreciate their design qualities. All the things regarded as traditional were taken as the new yardstick. Architects seized upon traditional building materials and techniques. Tiles, rubble masonry, half-timbering, iron-framed, leaded windows with lead glazing, and steep thatched roofs became acceptable. In the country, houses were built with steep, long roofs, many dormer windows and tall narrow chimneys.

Even now, this image of a country house is a very attractive one for many English people and the traditional-style cottage is still an ideal. A contrasting, modern or extravagant style has never really gained ground in England. Apart from improvements to technical installations, the old country houses were never modernized – in other words, they were never updated to a new style.

Garden design of this time also returned to older, traditional forms. People rediscovered the charm of simple flowers, the beauty of orchards and kitchen gardens, and began to appreciate the design quality of garden walls made of stone or slate.

The followers of the Arts and Crafts movement held up life in the country as the ideal. Towns and cities were seen as inevitable but ultimately undesirable environments. The goal of all architectural effort was to design a house in the country, from cottages through to manor houses. Such houses always had a garden and together they formed a unit. In general, garden design was in the hands of the architect, and, at around the turn of the century, the country house garden became an important aspect of garden design in general.

Paradoxically, the ideal of life in the country was connected with one of the main achievements of the machine age, one that was highly criticized by the advocates of the country life – the railway. In the late 19th century the suburban railway system around London was expanded. The still quite poor and thinly populated counties to the south and south-west of London – Kent, Sussex, Surrey, Hampshire, Berkshire – now had a rail link to the metropolis and soon developed into desirable residential areas. Land for building was still relatively cheap. Conditions were thus ripe for creating the kind of country homes people wanted in places that were convenient for their lifestyles. The owners of the new houses were not the landed gentry, who had already been in possession of grand manor houses with gardens and parks for generations; the new owners were members of the upper middle class. As businessmen, industrialists or lawyers they had achieved wealth in the city and were now looking for an appropriate country setting to suit their new status. The money to finance these housing projects had been made in the City, not in the country, as had been the case, for example, with the owners of early Renaissance villas in Italy. The professional lives of these new country people continued to be tied up with the City, with the result that the working members of a family had to commute to the capital each day. Long journeys came to be accepted, a circumstance that has changed little to this day. Most English people still regard the town or city as a necessary evil, whereas, for the well-off, the good life means a place in the country, close to nature.

The monthly magazine, *Country Life*, which was first published in 1887, played a major part in spreading this ideal of rural existence. Like other art magazines on the Continent, it was very well designed and it influenced the style of a whole epoch. *Country Life* was not only concerned with architecture and art, but also with various country themes, such as hunting, shooting, breeding dogs and horses, botany and gardens. Occasionally, articles appeared about historic gardens in Italy and France. Mainly, however, the houses and gardens featured were the many new country houses with formal gardens that were springing up all around England at the time. Foremost among these, and described in great detail, were all the new works carried out by the architect Edwin Lutyens. Edwin Hudson, the publisher of *Country Life*, was a personal friend of Lutyens and in 1899 he commissioned him to redesign and extend his country house in Berkshire.[18]

The Studio, which first appeared in 1894, took the same themes as *Country Life*, but its emphasis was more on arts and crafts. Both journals were well known in art and architecture circles, not only in Britain, but also on the Continent and in America. Through these channels the latest trends in English architecture and garden design reached a worldwide audience.

Around the turn of the century many books were also published about the new English country houses, their gardens and life in the country. Painters in particular paid great attention to these themes, capturing the ideals on canvas and generally sensitizing tastes. A whole generation of English painters produced small-format watercolours depicting country-house gardens. Although carried out with great skill, these paintings now seem too cloying and colourful to current tastes. Yet perhaps the work of these artists to some extent reflects the ideals of their time.

The garden movement that arose around 1900 reached all classes of society. Although the majority of the gardens in this book are, or were, owned by well-off members of the upper classes, many of the design ideas rapidly filtered down to ordinary people, albeit adapted to a much more modest scale. The herbaceous borders of the large country house were soon reproduced in miniature in the gardens of the working class. The new garden cities turned the terrace house with its little garden into a standard for a wide spectrum of British society.

The Formal Garden as Architectural Space

Nothing is as satisfactory than to see the well-designed and well-organised garden of the large country house, whose master loves his garden, and has good taste and a reasonable amount of leisure.
GERTRUDE JEKYLL, 1899[19]

A formal garden is set out according to a clear ground plan; in other words it is *constructed* in line with geometric principles and proportional relationships. The evidence that the abstract world of geometry has been imposed on nature is testimony to man's intervention and only when this is apparent has nature been transformed into a *garden*.

According to their own statements, practitioners of the new style of garden design emerging at the end of the 19th century based their ideas, on the forms used in the 17th century. The gardens were now much smaller, but the development of the ground plan followed the same principles. In its ideal form the garden was rectangular in overall plan, and divided up into a simple, regular structure made up of various different sections. It surrounded the country house on three sides, the fourth side having an entrance courtyard, or forecourt. The house and garden were set in the midst of charming countryside, and where possible a tree-lined avenue marked the approach.

The individual sections of the garden were also laid out on a rectangular, preferably square plan. This was then further broken down into geometric figures. Circles, squares and paths crossing or running diagonally were the most popular elements in the ground plan. Similar ground plans are known from classical antiquity. They are also found in medieval monastery courtyards, Renaissance gardens and in garden design in the Middle East. Even in the 20th century this overall scheme is still very much used; it is a template of garden design in the West. Such a plan always has a centre, which is generally emphasized by means of devices like sundials, ponds or statuary. The creation of a central focus and a clearly demarcated boundary lend a certain meditative calm to the garden.

By giving each area of the garden its own theme, the overall effect is one of variety and interest. The placing of garden areas with different functions in juxtaposition to each other allows each individual space to have its own, quite separate, often very striking design, but this is very far removed from the artistically designed spatial sequences evident in Italian Renaissance gardens.

Around 1900 a whole range of publications appeared in England about the great gardens of Italy. The superiority of the ground plans of the Villa d'Este and Villa Lante, for example, was immediately appreciated. Garden designers again discovered the power of the axis, which had been such an important design tool in Renaissance and Baroque gardens. They attempted to incorporate the axis in their design repertoire, but were seldom successful in establishing a convincing spatial sequence. Only Edwin Lutyens managed to create ground plans that allowed a satisfactory, artistically planned sequence of spaces. Gledstone Hall in Yorkshire, designed by Lutyens in 1922, is a fine example of this. More characteristic of garden design in the 20th century, however, are ground plans that are neither unintegrated additions nor axially arranged spatial sequences. The axis here no longer has the job of linking individual areas, but it becomes an independent element in its own right. It is the extrovert counterpart to the introvert garden space focused on its own centre. A close look at many of the gardens shown in the second part of this book will generally reveal a loose structure comprising individual garden spaces and a few axes reaching out in random directions.

A less-rigid arrangement of this kind inevitably gives rise to various non-geometrically shaped sections of garden. These areas were ideal for a naturalistic garden style. As we see in Hidcote Manor and Sissinghurst Castle, it is a combination that can be most successful, enriching the overall effect.

This general analysis of ground plan structure and the following systematic look at individual design elements can only hope to focus on certain aspects of a garden. A truly great garden will always have some secret essence that eludes analysis. Gertrude Jekyll maintained that a garden had to have one general idea, by which she most probably meant the specific quality, difficult to describe in words, that arises out of the *genius loci* and the inventiveness of the designer.[20]

16 Ground plan of a model country house by C.J. Kay, *c.* 1905. Hedges and walls divide the garden into separate spaces with different functions (redrawn from old plans).

17 View of the house from the garden. The house and garden form a single architectural unit.

18 Street elevation of the house. The H-shaped ground plan of the house creates a small entrance court at the front and at the back space for a sheltered terrace overlooking the garden.

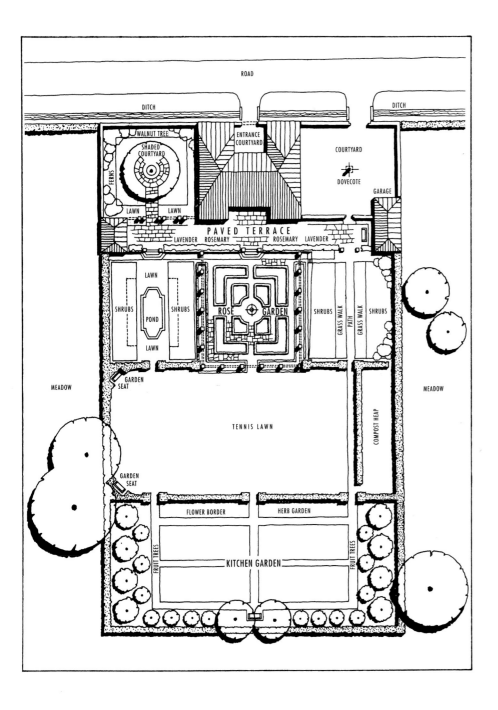

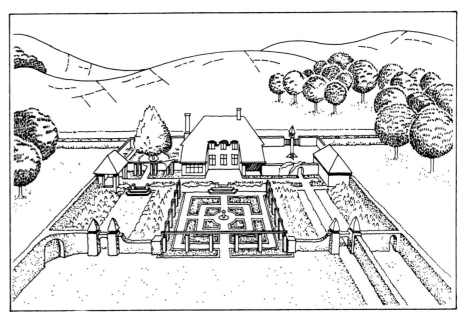

19 Bodnant Garden near Tal-y-Cafn Wales. The geometric volumes of the yew hedges have both sculptural and architectural effect in defining the garden space.

20 Ditchley Park, Enstone, Chipping Norton, in Oxfordshire. The strictly formal garden, bordered on two sides by pleached limes, was created in 1933 to plans by Sir Geoffrey Jellicoe.

Trees

Men seldom plant Trees till they begin to be Wise, that is, till they grow Old and find by Experience the Prudence and Necessity of it. When Ulysses, after a ten-years Absence, was return'd from Troy, and coming home, found his aged Father in the Field planting of Trees, He asked him, why (being now so far advanc'd in Years) he would put himself to the Fatigue and Labour of Planting that which he was never likely to enjoy the Fruits of? The good old Man (taking him for a Stranger) gently reply'd: I plant (says he) against my Son Ulysses comes home.
JOHN EVELYN, 1664 [21]

In the landscape garden trees were the most important element of composition. Designers were skilled in placing and grouping them in such a way that their beauty could be appreciated from any point. In the formal garden, too, trees are a fundamental component of the design. Although in many cases, as a feature standing outside the architectural order, trees can have a very pleasing effect of counterpoint, here we are specifically interested in their use to articulate space.

One of the most effective ways of placing

21 Trees.
a) Willersey Court, Gloucestershire, designed by the architect, Andrew Prentice, in 1909. Columnar yews emphasise the layout of the garden.
b) Pentillie Castle, Cornwall.
c) The Green, Cumbria.
d) Apple-tree walk at Penshurst Place, Kent.
e) Badminton House, Avon, South Gloucestershire.
f) Space-defining edge of a wood at Blickling Hall, Norfolk.
g) Hidcote Manor Garden, Gloucestershire. Specimen beech tree at the end of the Theatre Lawn.
h) Yew avenue in the garden of Montacute House, Somerset.
i) Greywalls, East Lothian, Scotland, designed by Sir Edwin Lutyens, 1901. Specimen tree in the centre of a semi-circular garden space.

a

b

c

d

e

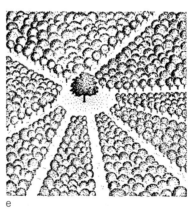

f

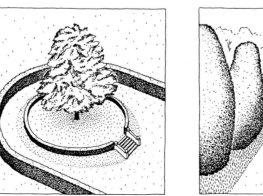

g

h

i

22 Tatton Park near Knutsford in Cheshire. Tree-lined avenues and rows of trees were already a characteristic feature of country-house gardens of the 17th century.

23 One of the most beautiful examples of the deliberate placement of a specimen tree is found in the garden of Hidcote Manor Garden near Chipping Campden in Gloucestershire. This fine old beech rises at the end of a large lawn. Raised as if on a platform and enclosed within a yew hedge this majestic tree stands displayed like a natural masterpiece. It makes such an impressive picture that it can also be used as a stage backdrop. In the summer months regular theatre performances take place on the steps in front of the tree (see Fig. 179).
(Unfortunately, we recently learned that this handsome beech had to be cut down in 1996.)

24 Newby Hall and Gardens, near Ripon in North Yorkshire. In parks and parkland the trees are generally planted far enough apart to enable them to grow into splendid specimens.

25 Bateman's, near Burwash in East Sussex. A row of pleached limes is one of the finest elements in this garden design. Rudyard Kipling created the garden in 1910 and today it is in the hands of the National Trust.

26 Lime-tree avenue at Ashdown House, near Lambourn, Berkshire.

trees is the tree-lined alley. As shown in the engravings in *Britannia Illustrata*, avenues and rows of trees were already a characteristic feature of country-house gardens in the 17th century. Trees were used not only to line the approach roads to the house, but also to border both sides of paths within the garden. The simplicity and clarity of the many lime and beech-tree avenues at Tatton in Cheshire (see Fig. 22) has a very grand, majestic effect. The chestnut avenue at Anglesey Abbey, Cambridgeshire is another very impressive sight, where, despite their considerable dimensions, the trees are only 50 years old. In May this part of the garden is filled with the glorious sight of thousands of 'candles'; in summer, with a canopy of beautifully shaped five-lobed leaves; and in autumn with splendid yellow and gold foliage – thus providing a wonderful natural spectacle all year round. Two sphinxes stand guard over the entrance to this avenue, and one reason why it is so impressive is that the trees are planted in three rows, with the middle row offset to fill the gaps. This arrangement gives a particularly dense boundary and a clear distinction between the trunks and crowns of the trees in the first row. The trunks remain clearly visible, as in avenues with single lines of trees, creating the same effect as a row of columns around an architectural space. A clearly delineated space is formed, and spatial depth is emphasized by the receding lines of tree trunks. To complete the effect, the rows of trees at the back have branches reaching down to the ground.

Happily, tree-lined avenues are still being planted in many English gardens, in particular in the properties of the National Trust. Often, this is not merely a case of reinstating what once was there, or of replacing fallen trees; the intention is also to add something appropriate to the historic setting. Some years ago, a new alley was planted at West Green House in Hampshire, a property owned by the National Trust. Its focal point at the end of the alley is a historicist column designed by the architect Quinlan Terry, which carries an amusing and rather thought-provoking inscription in Latin.[22]

Trees achieve their effect in an alley through their association with each other. By contrast, an impressive effect can also be created through placing a specimen tree in isolation. Even in the woodcuts in *Hypnerotomachia Poliphili* we can see individual trees used as decoration or as a centrepiece to a garden.

One of the most beautiful examples of deliberate placement of a specimen tree is in the garden of Hidcote Manor (see Figs. 23 and 185). At the end of the fine Theatre Lawn, 30 by 100 metres (100 ft by 320 ft) in size, is an old and mighty beech tree. This magnificent tree stands framed by a yew hedge on a raised platform one or two steps above the level of the lawn, inviting us to admire its natural splendour.

The great charm of lines of cypresses in the Tuscan countryside or of poplars in Flanders and in some English counties is matched in garden design by rows of conical or pillar-shaped juniper bushes or yew trees. These slim, precisely contoured trees are strong rhythmical elements in gardens.

Trees are either planted along both sides of a path, as in the garden of Snowshill Manor (see Fig. 197), or enclosing a garden space on all four sides, like pillars around a patio. An example of the latter effect can be seen in the garden of Montacute House in Somerset (see Fig. 158). In most instances yew trees are used for this purpose, in particular columnar yews (*Taxus baccata fastigiata*).

These trees have a naturally dense growth but they are nevertheless often additionally protected from the effects of storms and kept in shape by tying their branches with fine wire.

Rows of pleached limes are a special feature of design work with trees (see Fig. 25). The clear, closed form of these rows makes them a particularly charming way of articulating space, and they are of great significance in the formal garden. Lawrence Johnston had pleached limes in his garden in Hidcote, Vita Sackville-West planted them in Sissinghurst, Geoffrey Jellicoe in Ditchley Park, and Russell Page in Longleat. The effect is always captivating. Pleaching has, of course, a number of advantages: growth is held in check and the shape stays virtually the same, while unwanted shading is avoided. It also practically eliminates any chance of the trees being blown down, as the trunks are exceptionally strong in relation to the size of the crowns. In the garden of Penshurst Place in Kent the lime trees were planted only quite recently. In the initial stages of pleaching the branches of the trees are trained along wires. At first this does not look very attractive but within just five years of planting the general picture is quite satisfying. The green wall grows together and creates a precise, space-defining effect.

In addition to the above-mentioned ways of using trees to define and articulate space, many varieties can feature as a valuable design element in gardens, by virtue of their flowers or foliage colour. The flowers of the chestnut tree, magnolia and the Japanese cherry are part of the spring decoration in almost all large gardens in England. Leaf colour, too, can be used for decorative effect, and not only in the already rich autumn palette.

27 Mottisfont Abbey Garden, near Romsey in Hampshire. These columnar yews, regularly spaced, together with a long row of lavender bushes, give articulation and rhythm to the space. Sir Geoffrey Jellicoe designed this area of the garden in 1936.

Hedges and Walls

Nothing gives a garden such a unified impression as its articulation by means of visible walls. They clarify and explain the overall spatial structure, and thus elevate the garden into a higher artistic sphere.
HERMANN MUTHESIUS, 1920[23]

In the formal garden, hedges and walls are the most important means of providing shape and structure. They give the garden a structural framework and impose architectural order. They also offer protection for people and plants against the ever-present wind, a protection that is essential for all garden activities in England.

Hedges and walls are used both to mark out the boundaries of a garden and to articulate space within it. Woodcuts, engravings and paintings show that perimeter walls were an important design element in gardens of the Middle Ages and of the 16th and 17th centuries.

In the second half of the 17th century, the gardens of country houses, as seen in the engravings in *Britannia Illustrata*, consisted of a series of walled spaces. Each distinct section of the garden, whether it was an artistically laid-out parterre, a lawn for ball games, a kitchen garden or an orchard, was surrounded by high walls. All of the

28 Hedges.
a) Nunnington Hall, North Yorkshire.
b) Garden gate in the village of Stow-on-the-Wold, Gloucestershire.
c) Nymans Garden, West Sussex.
d) Wickham Court, Kent.
e) Old Place, Sussex.
f) Penshurst Place, Kent.
g) Brockenhurst Park, Hampshire.
h) The yew walk at Sissinghurst Castle Garden in Kent. It is 80 metres (260 ft) long and just 1½ metres (5 ft) wide.
i) After a design by F.L. Griggs, 1909.

42

a

b

c

d

e

f

g

h

i

29 Anglesey Abbey, Lode, Cambridgeshire. This impressive space, called the Circular Temple Lawn, was created in 1953 according to plans by the owner of the garden, Lord Fairhaven. A thick yew hedge and ten Corinthian columns form an effective circular garden space, in the centre of which stands a replica of Bernini's *David*. The entrance to the temple lawn is guarded by two lions created in the 18th century in the famous lead foundry and workshops of Jan van Nost.

larger country houses had a walled forecourt. English garden design shows a very distinct preference for a clear spatial structure. The ground plans of country houses were even designed so as to give structure to the space around them: plans in the shape of a U, an E or an H were used not only in manor houses of the 15th to 17th centuries, but have also been used for country houses in the 20th century.

For structural reasons the 2- to 3-metre (6- to 10-ft) high garden walls, which are often very long, have to be braced at regular intervals by piers. These also have the effect of optically articulating the walls. On the outside of the walls around older kitchen gardens or orchards one often finds substantial bricked abutments. Here the aim was not so much to create an optical effect as to provide a suitable, uninterrupted surface on the inside of the walls for growing espalier-trained fruit trees. One interesting way of overcoming the structural problems of wind pressure on long, high walls can often be found in orchards in Suffolk and also in Scotland. Here, the walls form a wavy line in plan, and therefore need no additional bracing from piers or abutments. They are known as crinkle-crankle walls.

Generally, garden walls are made of brick, but in some counties the use of rubble masonry or large rounded stones, or a combination of both, is more common. Special attention is often given to the design of the top of the wall – it can be finished with an edge of natural stone, or capped with slates.

The walls always provide a suitable site for climbing plants. In his book, *The Art and Craft of Garden Making*, published in 1900, Thomas Mawson devoted a whole chapter to climbing plants. He recommended 40 different types of plant for growing up garden walls, and described

no less than 24 varieties of clematis and 36 of climbing rose.[24] Garden or house walls covered with climbing plants are a typically English passion.

In the formal gardens created in the 20th century, hedges are used more often than walls as a means of defining space. To visitors from other countries, they are a very characteristic feature of the English countryside, and beautifully maintained hedges are among the most noticeable features of English gardens.

Gardens enclosed within high hedges are not uncommon in French Baroque garden design, but on the Continent it is rare to find such fine examples as in England, where hedge-enclosed areas of a garden are either centred on a particular motif, for example a pond or a group of sculptures, or have a particular colour or plant theme.

In addition to these more introverted, contemplative gardens there are also the wide hedge walks focused outwards on a distant point. One of the most beautiful examples of this is the Long Walk at Hidcote Manor (see p. 176). The Serpentine Walk at Chatsworth House in Derbyshire (see Fig. 37) is also noteworthy. Jan Kip's engraving in *Britannia Illustrata* shows that at the beginning of the 18th century Chatsworth had extensive parterres, balustraded terraces, flights of steps, ponds and hedge mazes. In the mid-18th century practically all of these were transformed into a landscape garden. In the 20th century, however, many areas close to the house were redesigned in the formal style. The Serpentine Walk was created in 1950, its remarkable design being devised by the owner of Chatsworth, the Duchess of Devonshire, who was inspired by the wavy outline of the walls around Scottish orchards.[25] A comparison of the plan of the hedge (Fig. 36) with its finished form as seen

in Fig. 37 is a surprising and very impressive demonstration of one of the most important rules of human spatial perception: the line of the hedge, which appears only slightly wavy in plan, is transformed into a striking and charming spatial form through the effect of perspective foreshortening.

Hedges are favourite backdrops for herbaceous borders in formal gardens. The variety of colour and form in the beds is set against the uniform dark green of a yew hedge, as if framed in a passe-partout border. There is usually a strip of grass about a metre wide between the border and the hedge, to give easy access to the flowers at the back. This is also a convenient way of keeping the hungry roots of the hedge away from the soil in the beds.

During the 16th and 17th centuries Italian influence was seen in the choice of cypresses for hedging, but nowadays yew is the favourite, alongside hornbeam, box, ilex and privet. Yew trees have a very old cultural tradition in England reaching back to ancient times. These yew hedges, dark green, very dense, always healthy-looking and usually perfectly clipped, are one of the most impressive features of the English garden.

In general, such hedges are 2 to 3 metres (6 to 10 ft) high and 60 to 150 centimetres (2 to 5 ft) wide. In cross section they usually taper slightly towards the top. Because they fulfil an architectural function they are treated as architectural components. Often, they can be found planted in a semicircle to frame a garden seat or piece of sculpture. Door-like or even window-like openings show a particularly uninhibited treatment of hedges as architectural elements.

Nothing spoils the appearance of a hedge more than patchy or even bare sections, such as can occur in the lower part. The secret of a perfect

30 Anglesey Abbey, Lode, Cambridgeshire. Plan and section of a circular garden space surrounded by a hedge. Laid out in 1953.

31 Elevations and sections of common hedge forms.
a, b) according to designs by F.L. Griggs, *c.* 1910.
c) Knightshayes Court, near Tiverton, Devon.
d) Penshurst Place, near Tonbridge, Kent.
e) Great Dixter House and Gardens, near Northiam, East Sussex.
f) Wakehurst Place, near Haywards Heath, West Sussex.
g) Nymans Garden, near Haywards Heath, West Sussex.

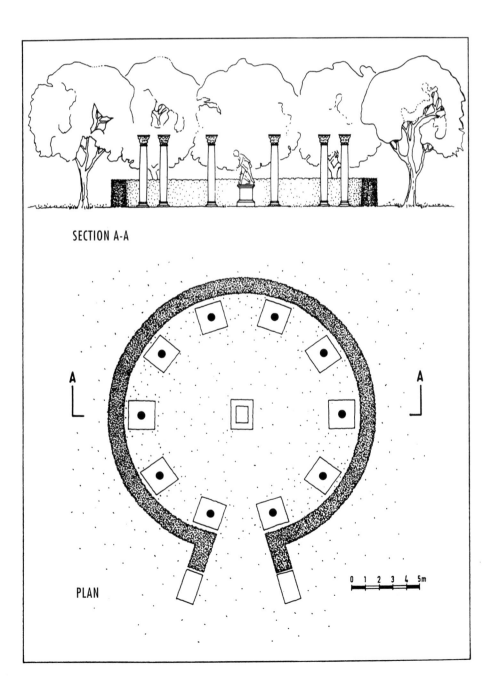

SECTION A-A

PLAN

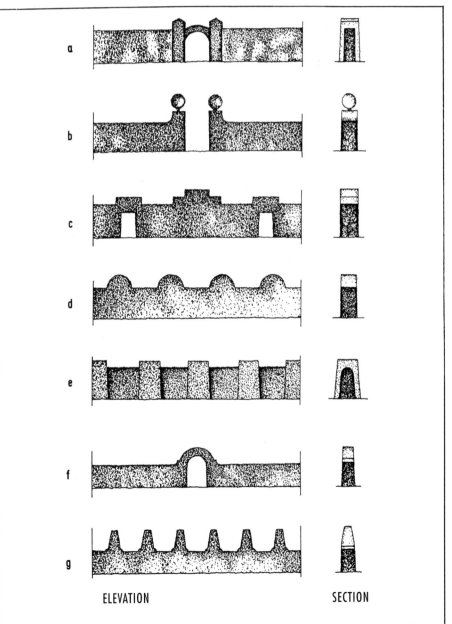

ELEVATION   SECTION

32, 33   Hedge around a small private garden in Chipping Campden in Gloucestershire. This freely shaped box hedge has the sculptural charm of a work of art.

34, 35 Great Dixter House and Gardens, near Northiam in East Sussex. The high, old yew hedges of this country-house garden designed by Sir Edwin Lutyens in 1910 are a model example of a beautiful, well-articulated hedge.

36 Plan and section of the hedge walk illustrated in the facing colour plate. A comparison of the two shows that the shallow curves of the hedge as seen on the plan have a much stronger effect when viewed from the ground, due to perspective foreshortening.

37 Chatsworth, Bakewell in Derbyshire. The Serpentine Walk, created in 1953, is bordered by high beech hedges laid out in a wavy line. This remarkable arrangement makes it one of the most original hedge designs this century.

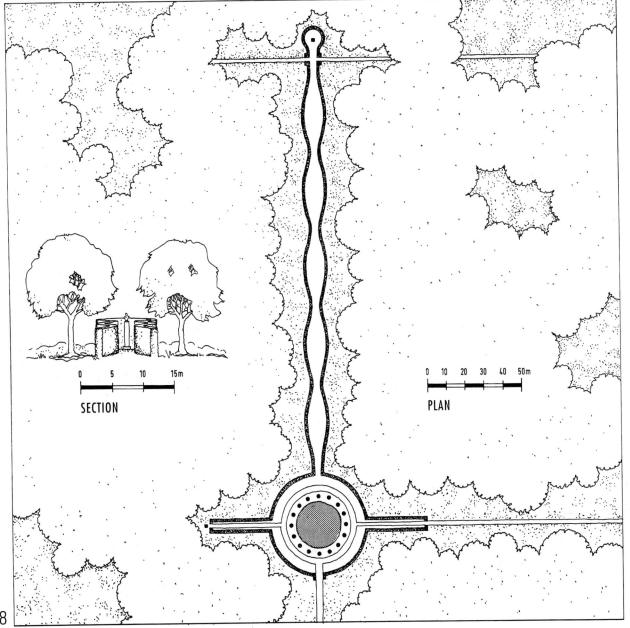

SECTION

PLAN

hedge is to make sure it has sufficient nutrients and adequate moisture; it must also be clipped into shape regularly, once or twice a year. Such trimming is not seen as a chore, but as skilled, precise craftsmanship.

There is a distinction between clipping and shaping, the latter being an altogether more elaborate process, involving marking out the line with string, and using a plumb line and template. Now and then it is necessary to patch the bare sections in a hedge by digging out the dead plants and replacing them with new ones.

Hedges are not for impatient gardeners. It takes years before they reach the desired shape. But once that shape is achieved they will, given correct care and feeding, remain a very valuable and attractive part of the garden for many decades. The splendid hedges of Penshurst Place in Kent (see pp. 168ff.) and of Arley Hall in Cheshire were planted around 1860. In the watercolours of George S. Elgood, painted around 1900, these gardens look very much as we see them today. The same is true of the gardens at Blickling Hall in Norfolk and Sudeley Castle in Gloucestershire – their hedges are as big and as wide as houses, and today they still look the same as they did in the early 1900s in the photographs that appeared in Gertrude Jekyll's book *Garden Ornament*. These hedges have thus kept a permanent shape for about a hundred years, and we can assume that they will retain it for a good few decades to come.

38–40 All three pencil drawings are taken from a series of essays that appeared between 1908 and 1910 in *The Studio* under the title of 'Architectural Gardening'. The author and illustrator was the architect Charles Edward Mallows.

41 Folly Farm, Sulhamstead in Berkshire. The extremely precise design of the walls in this garden was created in 1901 by Sir Edwin Lutyens.

Gateways

Pax intrantibus, salus exeuntibus
(Peace to all who enter, health to all who leave)
Inscription on the garden gate of Snowshill Manor in Gloucestershire

Where parts of the garden are enclosed by hedges and walls, gateways must be created to enable people to pass between them. In garden design, as in architecture, gateways are a favourite vehicle for artistic expression. The greatest attention is paid to the main entrance, as seen in the Renaissance gardens of Italy and in the English gardens of the 17th century. In both we find lavishly designed gateways guarded by stone lions and other heraldic animals to show all those who passed through that they were entering another world. But within the garden, artistically designed gateways were also erected to demarcate different areas.

Around 1900, the formal garden adopted the designs used in the 17th century, almost without alteration. There are many examples of a simple arch over an entrance of door-height, but in general the opening was designed as a proper gateway. Such gates are mostly flanked by

a

b

c

d

e

f

g

h

i

42 Gateways.
a) Breccles Hall, Norfolk.
b) Shrublands near Windermere in Cumbria, designed by Thomas Mawson in 1907.
c) Almshouses in Oundle, Northamptonshire.
d) In the village of Broadway, Hereford and Worcestershire.
e) Folly Farm, Sulhamstead in Berkshire, designed by Sir Edwin Lutyens in 1901.
f) Cleeve Prior Manor, Worcestershire.
g) Eyam Hall, Derbyshire.
h) Kinross House, Tayside Region in Scotland. Two cornucopias adorn the top of the wall and crown the garden gate.
i) Norman Chapel, Gloucestershire, after a design by Charles Robert Ashbee.

43 Great Dixter House and Gardens, near Northiam in East Sussex. As with all the gardens designed by Sir Edwin Lutyens, this one, dating from 1910, shows great skill in the treatment of gateways and other structural elements.

44 Design drawing by the architect Charles Edward Mallows. The illustration was published in 1909 in *The Studio*.

substantial piers, some of brick, others of natural stone, and some cut out of stately yew hedges. In line with classical tradition, the masonry piers are topped with some kind of stone statuary, either simple spheres, pine cones, acorns, sculptures or obelisks.

There exist many examples of masonry gate piers containing a semicircular arch-shaped niche of about a metre (3 ft) in height. It looks as if they may have been intended to display pieces of sculpture, but contemporary photographs show that this was not the case. So we can assume that these niches were built purely for their formal charm.

The garden gates themselves are mostly well crafted in oak and of a pleasing design. The wood is either left in its natural state to develop a silver-grey patina or it is painted. Although there are examples of solid wooden gates with no gaps, most gates have a solid frame infilled with spaced planking. Only the bottom section, which would otherwise allow cats, dogs and rabbits to slip through underneath, is solid. Wrought-iron gates are rare, and were used either for a very large gateway or in places where it was desirable to be able to see through the gate. In the period around 1900, when ironworking skills were very well developed and quite widespread, some excellent wrought-iron gates were produced, simple in form, but very effective.

Where hedges rather than walls border a garden, great attention is also paid to the design of the gateway. Here, the hedges themselves are often trained into the shape of gate piers, complete with spherical decoration at the top, mimicking the brick piers. Generally, however, hedge gateways consist of a narrow archway in the hedge itself. For extra emphasis the part of the hedge above the opening is often clipped into crenellations, as seen in the garden of Knights-

45 Design drawing by the architect Charles Edward Mallows. The illustration was published in 1910 in *The Studio*.

hayes in Devon and in Great Dixter in Sussex. Or, alternatively, as at Penshurst, the gateway can be crowned with a raised hedge arch.

It is not surprising that, in garden design, architects should pay special attention to the design of the gateway. Reginald Blomfield dealt at length with this topic. Thomas Mawson and Edwin Lutyens also considered it closely, and designed many examples that demonstrate their great artistic skill. They designed for shaped brick and produced some quite beautiful and imaginative examples. Gertrude Jekyll also underlined the significance of gateways as a design tool. In her book, *Garden Ornament*, published in 1918, no section is so richly illustrated as the chapter on gateways. She concentrates, however, almost exclusively on the entrance gateways of country houses of the 17th and 18th centuries, and pays scant attention to the equally carefully worked gateways of the smaller country houses that were being built around 1900. The latter were indeed inspired by the classical models seen in the older and grander properties, but their designers nevertheless managed to find a very convincing style and scale suited to the gardens of the middle and upper middle classes. Interestingly, Gertrude Jekyll stated quite clearly on a number of occasions that she considered it inappropriate to clad gate piers with ivy or other climbing plants.[26] She preferred to leave the form visible and thus better appreciated.

Many of the old garden gateways had an inscription. Above the gates of his garden, Charles Paget Wade had wooden plaques with epigrams inscribed upon them, and Sir Edward Phelips, who commissioned the wonderful Elizabethan gardens of Montacute House in around 1590, had the following inscription placed above the garden gate: 'Through this free opening none comes too early, none departs too late.'

46 Hazelby Garden, near Newbury in Berkshire. A solid, well-shaped, white-painted wooden gate leads into the kitchen garden.

47 Bampton Manor between Witney and Faringdon in Oxfordshire. The garden gates with their rather unusual diagonal struts are based on designs by William Chambers from the late 18th century. Chambers was inspired by traditional Chinese carpentry.

48 Knightshayes Court, near Tiverton in Devon. Where hedges are used to enclose spaces, it is logical that the entrances to these areas should also be cut out of the hedge.

49   Penshurst Place, near Tonbridge in Kent. The parts of the hedge above the openings are all shaped in this unusual way.

50   Great Dixter House and Gardens, near Northiam in East Sussex. The stepped shape of the hedge above the opening makes this gateway particularly impressive.

Terraces

*The terrace ... presents to the eye a solid found-
ation for the house to start from, and gives the
house itself greater importance ...*
REGINALD BLOMFIELD, 1892[27]

The idea of a terrace as a link between the house
and garden originated in Italian Renaissance
gardens. Italian villas of that period were built on
slopes, and the terrace was intended to provide
a pleasant, airy spot outside the house from
which to view the garden and the surrounding
countryside.

In England, however, country houses tended
to be built in wooded valleys and hollows, which
offered protection from the wind. Yet, despite the
quite contrasting conditions, designs for English
houses imitated Italian Renaissance villas with
their terraces, balustrades and flights of garden
steps. Almost all of the 17th-century gardens
depicted in the engravings in *Britannia Illustrata*
have these features.

The advantages of this scheme were readily
appreciated: not only did a terrace enhance the
setting of the house and provide a convenient link
between the house and garden, there were also
distinct practical benefits to the construction
process. Excavating a site and disposing of the
excavated earth was no small problem in the
days when all the work was done by hand, yet
house-owners were reluctant to surrender their
cellars. But constructing an artificially raised
terrace around the building made it unnecessary
to dig deep foundations and the excavated
material could also be used in the foundations

51 This isometric projection shows the main part of the
garden of Upton House in Warwickshire. The spatial order
of the house extends into the surrounding landscape
through two narrow terraces adjoining the building and a
terrace-like expanse of lawn.

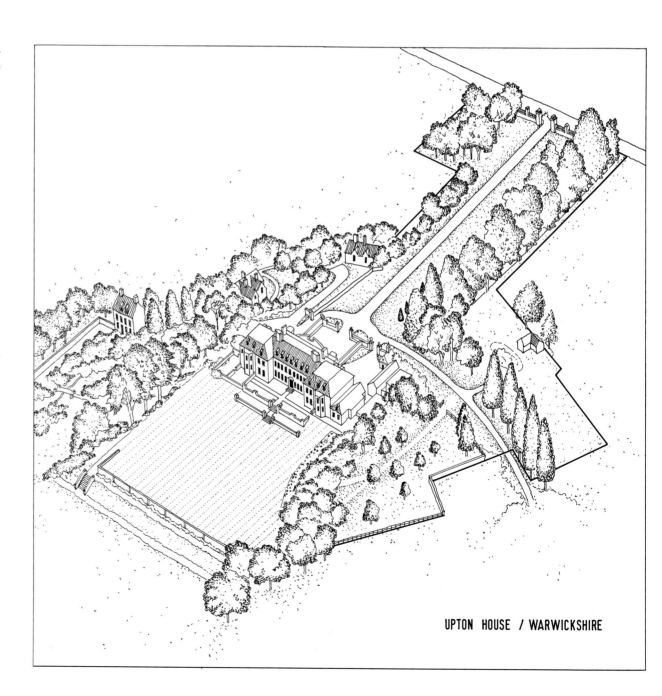

UPTON HOUSE / WARWICKSHIRE

52 Upton House in Warwickshire. In 1927 a terrace was added on the garden side, thus creating an important transitional element between the house and the garden.

53 The garden terrace of Craig-y-Parc house in South Wales. This pencil drawing, which appeared in 1913 in *The Studio*, is by the architect Charles Edward Mallows.

of the terrace. Another advantage of this arrangement was that the cellars remained drier.

Most country houses built in the 18th century, in the era of the landscape garden, dispensed with the terrace. This was a decidedly weak point in the design of the landscape garden. If a building has no adjoining terrace, then it lacks a most useful outdoor space where people can sit; it has no transition zone between inside and outside, where one is outdoors, yet still in the shelter of the building. This can be felt very strongly, for example, at Petworth House, the famous country house set in a landscape garden designed by

Capability Brown. When seen from a distance this large, clearly articulated building forms a charming and effective contrast to the surrounding landscape, but, viewed from close to, the lack of a terrace as a connecting link is evident. There is no space outside, in front of the building, from which to view the grand panorama of the landscape garden.

The designers of the late 18th century were well aware of this problem and the advocates of the landscape garden made their first concessions. In his book, *Landscape Gardening*, published in 1803, the garden designer Humphrey Repton suggested laying out a garden in the formal style next to the house. The terrace was the first element of the formal garden to be reintroduced and by the end of the 19th century it had become an established design feature.

In the formal garden of around 1900 the terrace was the focus and starting point for the entire plan of the garden. Writing in 1920, Hermann Muthesius, who had been greatly influenced by the gardens created in England at the beginning of the 20th century, stated, 'The formation of a terrace is an artistic function of the highest order. The terrace is particularly welcome placed immediately in front of the house so that one goes directly outside from the ground floor of the house, without going up or down steps. The garden proper then begins at the edge of the terrace. Uneven land is no real obstacle to the garden designer. On the contrary, it gives him an opportunity to create a harmonious and pleasing arrangement. Instead of using retaining walls for the edges of the terrace it is also possible to use embankments. However, it is well known that

embankments are difficult to plant, and especially difficult if one wants to grass them over. The outline of an embankment is also too soft and indefinite to lend any real clarity to the design of the garden.'[28]

Muthesius saw the terrace not only as an element connected with the house, but also as an ideal means of articulating the garden and ordering topographical conditions. In this, too, the English formal garden corresponds to the model of the Italian Renaissance garden.

Another aspect must also be considered: the retaining walls of the terrace are an ideal place for planting rockery perennials, and if height allows, even climbing or twining plants. Walls also form a very good backdrop to the linear herbaceous borders.

Some of Kip's engravings from *Britannia*

Illustrata show isolated terraces, standing separated from the main house at the end of a section of garden. There are also garden paths, raised several metres above the general level of the garden to give a good view of a parterre garden or a bowling green (see p. 134). Very few such isolated terrace structures from the 17th century survive in England, but we can gain a good impression of what they were like in the garden of Athelhampton House, where, in 1893, the architect Inigo Thomas designed a garden terrace modelled on 17th-century examples. This terrace is still very well preserved, but unfortunately it lacks any real function. It is difficult to tell whether such features ever did have a function. In such a situation the terrace is nothing more than a highly elaborate, purely formal element.

54 A wide garden terrace surrounds the entire house. The design is also by Mallows and appeared in *Country Life* in 1912.

55 Athelhampton House Gardens, near Puddletown in Dorset. Examples of terraces isolated from the main house are also found in engravings from the 17th century. In 1893, Inigo Thomas was inspired by these earlier models in his design for the garden of Athelhampton House.

56 Jenkyn Place near Bentley in Hampshire. The terrace extends across the whole width of the house and, with its elegant outline, forms an impressive link between house and garden.

Garden Steps

It is the garden steps and their connection with the terrace that enable architecture to reach out into the garden and link it with the house.
MARIE-LUISE GOTHEIN, 1914[29]

The motif of garden steps as a design element was first developed in the early 16th century by Donato Bramante in his new design for the Belvedere Garden at the Vatican Palace. Since then it has been an integral part of garden design.[30] The steps motif was such a significant innovation in spatial organization that the Belvedere Garden became a landmark in the history of garden design. The idea of two flights of steps branching symmetrically left and right from a joint base, and coming together again at the top is a basic theme that has been used in countless gardens over hundreds of years. Skilfully designed garden steps formed one of the most important features of Renaissance and Baroque gardens.

57 Steps.
a) Ladham House, Kent.
b) Polesden Lacey, Surrey. A yew hedge forms the 'railing' to the steps.
c) Court House, Gloucestershire.
d) Folly Farm, Sulhamstead in Berkshire, designed by Sir Edwin Lutyens in 1901.
e) Greenwood in East Sussex, designed by Thomas Mawson in 1908.
f) Orchards in Surrey, designed by Sir Edwin Lutyens in 1899.
g) The Priory, Gloucestershire.
h) Ashby St. Ledgers, Northamptonshire, designed by Sir Edwin Lutyens in 1904.
i) Eyford House, Gloucestershire.

58 Charleston Manor at West Dean, near Eastbourne in East Sussex. Often garden steps are laid out in the shape of a semicircle. This gives a particularly sculptural effect.

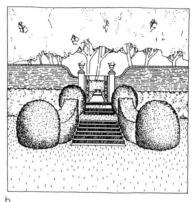
a

b

c

d

e

f

g

h

i

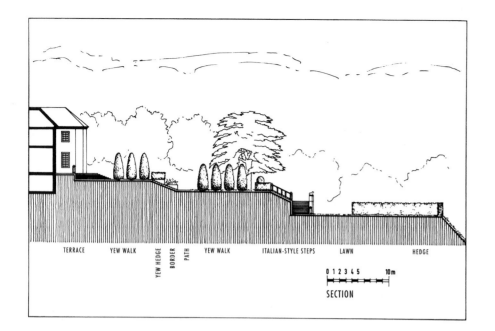

TERRACE   YEW WALK   YEW HEDGE   BORDER   PATH   YEW WALK   ITALIAN-STYLE STEPS   LAWN   HEDGE

0 1 2 3 4 5   10m

SECTION

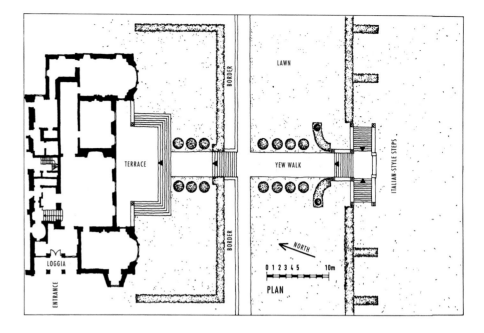

BORDER   LAWN

TERRACE

YEW WALK   ITALIAN-STYLE STEPS

LOGGIA

BORDER

ENTRANCE

NORTH

0 1 2 3 4 5   10m

PLAN

Engravings and paintings from the 17th century (see Fig. 13) show that Italian-style garden steps were also adopted in England. However, as the sites for new gardens were generally not as steep as in Italy, the dimensions of the steps were always more modest. In Italy, on the other hand, garden steps were becoming ever more flamboyant and, for today's tastes, too ostentatious.

In the landscape gardens of the 18th century the topography of the terrain was not dealt with by means of terracing, but through graduating the inclines. Thus garden steps lost their function and became a superfluous feature of garden design.

In the formal garden of around 1900 the motif of garden steps was again taken up. Although Reginald Blomfield and Inigo Thomas, in their book, *The Formal Garden in England*, devote only a short paragraph to garden steps, and consider neither their origins nor their design possibilities, the illustration they use clearly shows an Italianate flight of steps; evidently they appreciated the special significance of the motif. Various designs created by Blomfield around 1900 also show flights of steps with balustrades and grotto niches, clearly oriented to Italian models.[31]

The architect Thomas Mawson also takes up this motif in his book, *Garden Craft Old and New*, published in 1901, where he presents designs that are all variations on the theme of Italian-style steps. However, only very few such steps were built, and then generally as an addition to historic

buildings rather than as part of an entirely new garden. The country houses built around 1900 were already much more modest in scale, and it was generally felt, quite rightly, that this grand style was rather inappropriate. Nevertheless, one or two examples of Italian-style steps from the turn of the century have survived – at places such as Parnham House in Dorset (see Fig. 167) and Hill of Tarvit in Scotland (see Figs. 61 and 62), both gardens that were created around 1910 .

More typical of the formal garden at this time were straight flights of steps bridging a height difference of 1 to 2 metres (3 to 6 ft). These flights either formed part of an ensemble with a retaining wall or they were set into embankments. The individual steps are always closed in at the sides and constitute a precise organizing element in the overall design of the garden. Brick or natural stone is generally used for the steps and they often have balustrades in the Italian style.

Smaller flights of steps are frequently laid out in a semicircular form to give a particularly sculptural effect. Interestingly, this favourite device in formal gardens can be traced back to the early designs of the 17th century and to Italian origins. Many such arrangements are to be seen in Kip's engravings.

These illustrations also show some very refined variations on the theme of circular steps laid out in a convexo-concave pattern. The lower steps are convex in shape and lead to a circular

intermediate landing from where they continue upwards in a concave shape. This, too, is originally an Italian Renaissance design. Examples can be found in urban areas, such as those in the town of Lucignano in Tuscany, and in Renaissance gardens, such as that of the Villa Lante near Viterbo.[32] In the formal garden of around 1900 convexo-concave steps cropped up again and again as an element of the design. Edwin Lutyens produced a wide range of variations on this motif.

In the context of Italian Renaissance gardens we have already noted the significant connection between garden steps and the fact that from the 16th century onwards garden design in the whole of Europe was in the hands of architects. Planners of formal gardens in England also approached the task of designing garden steps with great energy and imagination. Yet in many cases one is forced to conclude that the results did not entirely equal the effort expended.

All too easily the architect is tempted to overdo things when designing a garden. Too much stonework, no matter how cleverly detailed, is unsatisfactory in a garden. Some of Lutyens's gardens confirm this, especially in those instances where the planting is no longer as luxuriant as originally intended. Except for those examples where a flight of steps is intended to mark a distinct break in the garden, or to form the main axis, retaining walls and steps should never exceed 1.60 metres (5½ ft), in other words, head height.

59, 60   The garden steps at Hill of Tarvit, near Cupar, Fife, Scotland, are seen here in section and plan.

61, 62   Hill of Tarvit, near Cupar, Fife, Scotland. This property is now owned by the National Trust for Scotland. The house and garden were designed by the Scottish architect, Robert Lorimer, in 1906. The steps are clearly modelled on those found in Italian Renaissance gardens.

63 Great Dixter House and Gardens, near Northiam in East Sussex. These steps, designed in 1910 by Sir Edwin Lutyens, are a very skilful design, both in terms of detail and overall integration into the garden.

64 Sissinghurst Castle Garden, near Cranbrook in Kent. The architectural order of the carefully constructed brick steps is continued in the yew hedges to create a very convincing effect.

65 Folly Farm, Sulhamstead in Berkshire. These small steps, designed by Sir Edwin Lutyens in 1901, also show a very effective combination of yew hedges and brickwork.

Garden Paths

Paths are of especial importance in the appear-ance of a garden. They should be straight.
HERMANN MUTHESIUS, 1920[33]

Typically, among the main targets for the increas-ing criticism of the formal garden in the 18th century were the straight paths that the land-scapists claimed were 'unnatural'. The theorists of the landscape garden advocated paths that followed a winding course, insisting that nature itself preferred a curved line to a straight one.[34]

Reginald Blomfield and Inigo Thomas took up this point with vigour in 1892 in *The Formal Garden in England*: 'Now as a matter of fact in nature – that is, in the visible phenomena of the earth's surface – there are no lines at all; "a line" is simply an abstraction which conveniently expresses the direction of a succession of objects which may be either straight or curved. "Nature" has nothing to do with either straight lines or curved; it is simply begging the question to lay it down as an axiom that curved lines are more "natural" than straight ... and it is open to us to say that the natural man would probably prefer a straight path to a zigzag ...'[35]

Rather than stir up the old argument of what is natural and what is unnatural, we would like to propose the theory that the shape of a garden path is perceived to be beautiful and proper when we see a *reason* for it. If a path is curved and winding for no obvious reason, then we will instinctively reject it. If, however, the twists and turns are due to topographical, artificial or even

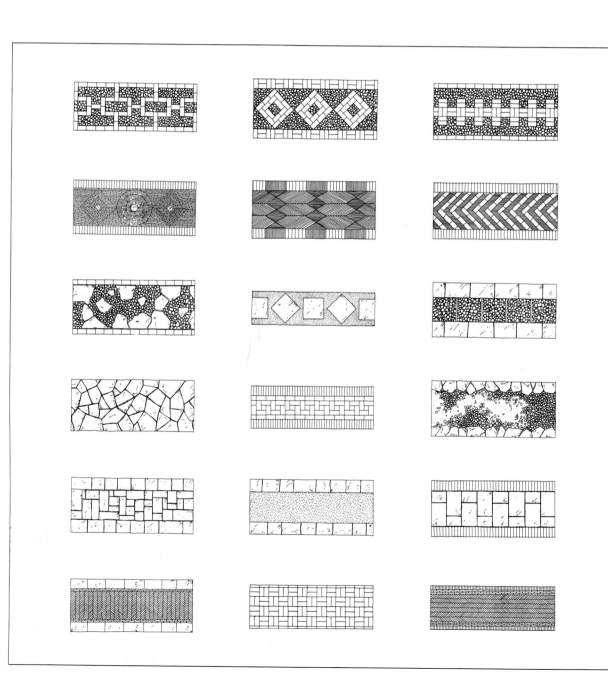

66 In the formal garden particular attention is paid to the design and construction of the surfaces for terraces and paths. Materials used include rectangular or irregularly shaped stone slabs, bricks or rounded pebbles. These are also used in combination to create geometric patterns.

67 Sissinghurst Castle Garden, near Cranbrook in Kent. The pretty brick pattern and the precise box hedges around the beds give an attractive look to this narrow garden path.

68–71 All four pencil drawings show very pretty and atmospheric garden paths. Charles Edward Mallows drew these illustrations for his series of articles on 'Architectural Gardening', which appeared in *The Studio* between 1908 and 1910.

artistic features, this is perceived to be sensible or picturesque. In formal gardens, most of which are considerably smaller in size than landscape gardens, the paths are always straight. The *reason* for this lies in the geometric dictates of the garden's structure. Although this is only an abstraction, it can be traced clearly in the spatial reality of the garden.

As in Italian Renaissance gardens the main

paths in English formal gardens always have a specific destination, whether that be a pond, a garden pavilion, a white-painted garden seat or a piece of sculpture.

A special feature of many English gardens of this century is the 'walk', a path that leaves the formal part of the garden and extends out, in a straight line, into the more freely laid out areas. One such example is the Long Walk at Hidcote Manor (see pp. 174ff.). The promise of a view of the open countryside maintains interest and tempts one along the relatively long and uniformly designed path.

Garden designers have always debated the correct width for a path. Thomas Mawson[36] assumed 1.80 to 3.60 metres (6 to 12 feet); Hermann Muthesius recommended a width of

1.25 to 1.30 metres (4 to 4¼ ft), and noted that this would allow at least two people to walk abreast.[37] Clearly Muthesius had much more modest properties in mind than Mawson. The correct width of a garden path can only be derived from the overall context. In the White Garden at Sissinghurst (see p. 195, pp. 200ff.) some paths are just 60 centimetres (2 ft) wide; in Montacute House (see pp. 150ff.) they are almost five metres (16 ft).

In the formal garden special attention is always paid to the design and construction of the surfaces for terraces and paths. Gravel or chippings are used mostly for the main approach and the forecourt, but firmer surfaces are needed in the garden. Materials used include rectangular or irregularly shaped stone slabs, bricks or rounded pebbles. These are also used in combination to

create geometric patterns. Thomas Mawson, an architect who also designed gardens, Edwin Lutyens and Charles Edward Mallows all produced some very imaginative designs (see Fig. 66).

The edges of the path are always perfectly straight, but a popular habit is to blur this outline with plants, for example, by allowing low-growing perennials to spread a little way onto the path, or in some cases quite a long way. Mostly the paths are edged all along their length with pinks, thrift, saxifrage or lavender, as recommended by Gertrude Jekyll.[38]

Visitors from abroad, however, are struck particularly by the grass walks in English gardens. These walks, flanked by herbaceous borders or hedges, are planted with closely mown grass instead of being laid with stone flags. It is sheer delight to walk along these soft, well-tended carpets of lawn and one has to admit that they are far more beautiful than any stones, no matter how artistically arranged. The grass walks at the National Trust properties seem to lose nothing of their beauty even after hundreds of visitors have passed over them.

Grass walks have a long tradition in England, stretching back many hundreds of years. Even Francis Bacon mentioned them, if only to advise against them as being too damp. There is some truth in this, but in his day the grass was almost certainly not kept as short as it is today.

The paths in the formal garden generally have a particular theme, such as an iris walk, a lavender walk, an azalea walk or a lime walk. The decision to concentrate on a theme gives clarity to the design and it is a device that was also typical of Italian Renaissance gardens. There, however, plants were not the determining factor, but rather architectural and sculptural subjects. Nevertheless, a garden path like the *Viale delle cento fontane* in the Villa d'Este achieves its grandiose effect through a concentration on *one* theme.

72   Tirley Garth in Cheshire. A design by Charles Edward Mallows, *c.* 1909.

73   Tintinhull House Garden, near Yeovil in Somerset.

74   Marsh Court, near Stockbridge in Hampshire, designed by Edwin Lutyens in 1904.

75   Chilcombe House, near Bridport in Dorset.

76   Sissinghurst Castle Garden, near Cranbrook in Kent.

The Pergola

Grace ... had supposed all her life that vineyards were covered with pergolas ... heavy with bunches of hot-house grapes, black for red wine, white for champagne. Naboth's vineyard, in the imagination of Grace, was Naboth's pergola, complete with crazy paving underfoot.
NANCY MITFORD, 1951[39]

The impassioned gardeners of England will probably always regret that their climate does not allow them to grow vines with any great success. Although historic documents do record the presence of vineyards in Southern England during the Middle Ages and the Renaissance, the wine is likely to have been of poor quality. In recent times, however, vines are grown in many places in England, and English vineyards have achieved some good results. Anyone who has witnessed the great care with which rather modest vines are tended on some south-facing slopes in Kent, or seen Hampton Court's 250-year-old vine,[40] carefully protected in a greenhouse and by now almost a national monument, will wonder just why the vine of all plants has attracted so much attention. Perhaps it is a sure sense of the symbolic value and history of this plant, an appreciation that it was the vine that first taught man that nature needs the caring hand of the gardener in order fully to unfold. For this reason it has become the very symbol of gardening. The many and varied Christian and religious associations have also played a part in strengthening our admiration for the vine.

For the English, much more than for any other

77 Pergola-like climbing frames along a path up to a country house. In 1909 the architect Baillie Scott illustrated his design for a country house near Guildford in Surrey with this watercolour.

nation north of the Alps, a vine-clad pergola heavy with bunches of grapes is the epitome of the south with its long summers and abundance of light. Countless paintings show that, for the English, among the most vivid memories of their beloved Italy were the pergolas. The pergolas on the Costa Amalfina and on Capri were a favourite motif for English painters. The garden painter, George S. Elgood, and several of his contemporaries also depicted pergolas in their work.[41]

It was generally recognized that the pergola came from Italy. William Robinson and Reginald

78 Marsh Court, near Stockbridge in Hampshire, built in 1904. In Sir Edwin Lutyens's country-house projects pergolas are frequently used as a link and transitional element between the house and the garden.

Blomfield mentioned this explicitly, and the latter wrote, 'Pergola is, of course, Italian, and signified originally a trellis of wood at the sides and overhead, supported at the angles by stone piers and pillars; over this trellis was trained the vine, to form a green arbour.'[42]

Old paintings and woodcuts show that modest versions of the pergola were already common in English gardens in the Middle Ages and particularly in the gardens of the 16th and 17th centuries.[43] In the landscape garden of the 18th century, however, they had lost all meaning as a design element, which led Blomfield to lament that 'Few examples of older pergolas remain. They were ruthlessly swept away by the landscape gardeners ...'[44]

In the formal garden of the 20th century pergolas again became an important feature. In addition to their role in organizing space, and acting as a charming reference to Mediterranean gardens, another aspect came to the fore: the pergola offered a very suitable and impressive trellis for the many climbing plants that were becoming more and more popular in gardens at the end of the 19th century. Plants such as the many varieties of the climbing rose, or clematis, wisteria, jasmine and honeysuckle, buzzing with bees, all found the perfect spot there. As this is now, in fact, the most important aspect of a pergola, and not, as in the south, the necessity of providing a shady path, English gardens often have a succession of single climbing posts instead of a walkway that is entirely covered over.

William Robinson, otherwise a strict opponent of the formal garden, was very much in favour of the pergola and set out one or two design rules that are still valid today.[45] Firstly, he stipulated that, for best effect, a pergola should only be used on main paths in the garden. Secondly, he maintained that it should lead to a particular focal point. And indeed, pergolas work best if they arrive at a seat, a summerhouse or a viewing point. Also, no tall trees should be in the vicinity of the pergola, Robinson's reason being that their roots would take absorb the nutrients needed by the climbing plants. To this consideration, which is fully justified from the gardening point of view, we must add the design note that neighbouring high trees compete optically with the pergola and diminish its effect. Finally, Robinson recommended that the form of a pergola should be clear and simple.

Even today, more than one hundred years after Robinson warned against the questionable prettifying efforts of the 'rustic carpenter', we are in full agreement with him. Here, he was referring to the supposedly more 'natural' frame constructions, made of forked birch branches, which were particularly popular for summerhouses, pergolas and small bridges in the 19th century.

One of the most impressive pergolas in Britain is without doubt the laburnum arch of Bodnant Garden in Wales (see Fig. 81). For two to three weeks in May it is a splendid sight, and it is a rare pleasure indeed to walk under such a sea of golden blossom. The frame now serves less as a support for the laburnum trees, now grown to maturity, but more as a kind of restraining corset.

Bodnant Garden was probably the inspiration behind many other laburnum pergolas built in recent decades in Britain. Geoffrey Jellicoe planned one at Sutton Place and Rosemary Verey added one to the garden of Barnsley House. The owners of Folly Farm also created a laburnum pergola in their garden, which was originally designed by Edwin Lutyens.

The garden of Moseley Old Hall, a National Trust property, has an interesting pergola built entirely of oak beams (see Fig. 79). It was built in 1960 following designs taken from 16th-century woodcuts.

Some very good examples of well-designed pergolas, particularly in terms of their integration in the overall design, are to be found in the gardens of Gertrude Jekyll and Edwin Lutyens, for instance, the one at Little Thakeham, which, seen from the terrace, extends the central axis of the house and leads to a large orchard; or the one at Hestercombe Garden, which forms a distinct spatial break at the end of the garden, and at the same time frames the view of the surrounding countryside (see Fig. 191).

Jekyll's and Lutyens's pergolas are almost all of the classical mould: pillars of brick or natural stone, topped with a frame of oak. Gertrude Jekyll wrote, 'I do not like a mean pergola, made of stuff as thin as hop poles ... No, a pergola should be more seriously treated, and the piers at any rate should be of something rather large – either oak stems 10 inches [25 cm] thick, or better still, of 14-inch [35-cm] brickwork painted with limewash to a quiet stone colour.'[46]

79 Moseley Old Hall, near Wolverhampton in Staffordshire. This oak pergola was constructed in 1960 to designs taken from 16th-century woodcuts.

80 Barnsley House, near Cirencester in Gloucestershire. The laburnum walk is one of the most beautiful design features in this recently created country house garden. Growing at the foot of the laburnum trees are ornamental onion plants with pale lilac flowers (*allium aflatunense*). The combination of lilac with the strong yellow of the laburnum may be rather adventurous, but as no other colour is allowed to conflict, the effect has great charm.

81 Bodnant Garden near Tal-y-Cafn in Wales. The laburnum arch in this garden is one of the most impressive sights in British gardens. For two to three weeks in May it presents a most spectacular show.

Knot Gardens and Parterres

Of all the best ornaments used in our English gardens, knots or mazes were the most ancient, and at this day of most use among the vulgar, the least respected with great ones.
GERVASE MARKHAM, 1615[47]

One of the questions that always arises in formal garden design is the matter of how to mark out the beds. Clear, permanent boundaries are needed to accentuate the intended artistic form. In the Middle Ages the beds were bounded by wooden planking or wickerwork and raised slightly above the level of the paths. In Renaissance gardens edging of box or other small-leaved shrubs became more and more popular. Regular clipping kept them low and well shaped, and encouraged dense growth. From very early on people saw an opportunity here for inventiveness and began to lay out geometric edging patterns. Soon the

82 Parterres.
a) Balcarres, Fife, Scotland.
b) Ashdown House, Berkshire. The small box parterre was reconstructed in 1955. It creates a pretty transition from the house to the lime-tree avenue reaching out into the wide landscape.
c) Pitmedden, Grampian, Scotland, reconstructed parterre.
d) Little Moreton Hall, Cheshire, reconstructed parterre.
e) Moseley Old Hall, near Wolverhampton in Staffordshire, reconstructed parterre.
f) Abbotswood, near Stow-on-the-Wold, Gloucestershire, designed by Sir Edwin Lutyens.
g) Great Fosters, Surrey. This parterre, interspersed with topiary, was created in 1918.
h) Barnsley House, Gloucestershire. One of the few true knot gardens.
i) Cliveden, Buckinghamshire.

83 Mottisfont Abbey Garden, near Romsey in Hampshire. In 1938 the garden designer, Norah Lindsay, created this beautiful parterre marked out in box and lavender.

a

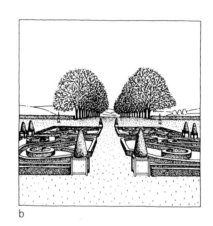
b

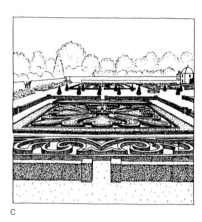
c

d

e

f

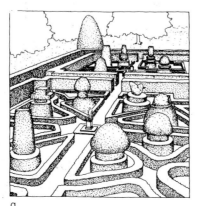
g

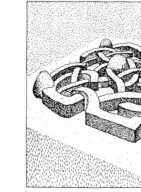
h

i

CE

graphic design of the edging to the beds became more important than what they contained. In French gardens of the 17th and 18th centuries a great deal of energy and imagination went into designs for this type of layout, which since the 18th century has generally been known as a parterre (from the French, meaning 'on even ground').

The oldest form of English parterre garden is the knot. Low hedges of box, hyssop, rosemary or lavender are planted in intertwining shapes around small beds to form decorative patterns. The beds themselves contain flowering or sweet-smelling plants. Beds of this type were one of the most important elements of English garden design in the 16th century. Even if knot gardens are generally considered to be a specifically English form of parterre design, it must be noted that the oldest known representation of a knot garden is to be found in the *Hypnerotomachia Poliphili*.[48] It is doubtful whether such knot-patterned beds were common in Italian Renaissance gardens, but it is unlikely that this woodcut was merely the product of imagination. Perhaps the origins lay in Arabic art, where such ornamental forms were already known.

All the works on garden theory that appeared in Italy, France and England in the 16th and 17th centuries contain pattern sheets for designing parterres. It is to be assumed, however, that not many of these graphically impressive forms would ever have been turned into a real garden. The earliest pattern sheets were produced by an Italian, Sebastiano Serlio, and dated 1537. The first comparable English designs were published in 1563 in *The Gardener's Labyrinth* by Thomas Hill. Further examples appeared at the beginning of the 17th century in the books of William Lawson and Gervase Markham. Even though the designs are

84 Design samples for knot gardens. The woodcuts are taken from *The Country Farm* by Gervase Markham, published in 1615.

very similar to the Italian models, a definite English preference for patterns composed of intertwining strips can be seen. Perhaps influences came from the art of decorative woven rushwork, which was highly developed in England and Ireland in the Middle Ages.

The two terms, parterre garden and knot garden, are often interchanged in English, but strictly speaking a knot garden refers to an intertwined pattern, whereas a parterre garden is understood as the generic term for all formal arrangements of beds.

The engravings in *Britannia Illustrata* and many 17th-century paintings show that another, very simple type of surface design was also used, in addition to the knot garden. Instead of using hedges, labour-intensive flower decoration or coloured gravel to form the outlines, patterns were formed by patches of lawn or gravel, with the contours marked out permanently in wood or metal set into the ground. Some indeed made an attractive graphical arrangement, but the general effect was rather flat and monotonous. In the instances where conical or ball-shaped trees were added, the composition become more satisfactory. This latter type of parterre design was adopted in Continental Europe and became known in French Baroque garden design as the 'parterre à l'anglaise'.

The parterres of 17th-century France were much more complicated than those of England. Artistic arabesque designs were filled with colourful plants or materials such as brick or marble chippings and even coal to form highly refined pictures. These bed designs looked like embroidery patterns, which is why in French they were called 'parterres de broderie'. Kip's engravings show that some of these ideas from France were taken up in England. Yet there were critics of this

86, 87   Inigo Triggs also included several pages of designs for knots and parterres in his work, *Formal Gardens in England and Scotland*, published in 1902. However, in the 20th century, such intricate designs have rarely been used. It seems as if the draughtsman has been more taken with the beauty of the graphic design than its practical application for gardening.

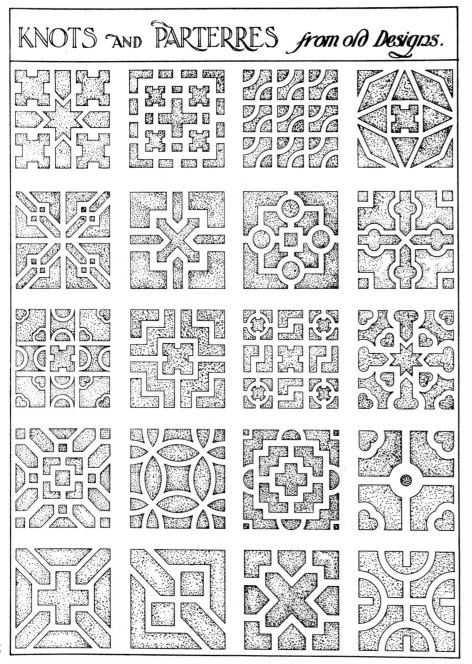

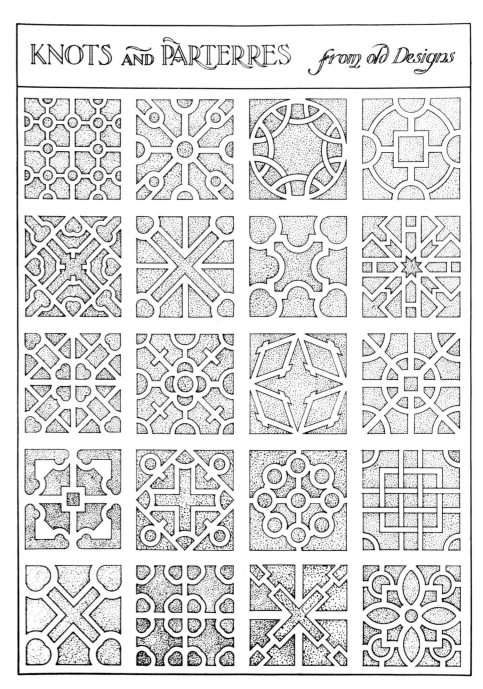

88, 89 Moseley Old Hall, near Wolverhampton in Staffordshire. In 1960 a parterre was reconstructed here in the style of the 17th century. Low box hedges, gravel surfacing and privet clipped into ball shapes present a very convincing picture.

fashion. Francis Bacon scoffed, 'As for the making of Knots or Figures with divers coloured Earths, that they may lie under the Windows of the House on that Side which the Garden stands, they be but Toys: you may see as good Sights many times in Tarts.'[49]

Most of the English parterre gardens were dug up in the 18th century. People were tired of the shapes and perhaps also of the work they entailed, and looked instead to a new design ideal in the landscape garden.

Parterres only slowly regained importance in the English formal garden of around 1900. Gertrude Jekyll devoted a whole chapter to them in *Garden Ornament*, but she seems not to have produced any designs for them herself. William Robinson roundly condemned the parterre, and even reviled box edging as 'a source of pointless labour' and 'a breeding place for insects'.[50]

The architects Thomas Mawson and Edwin Lutyens designed parterres in which the pattern was created mainly by the paving, and the plants occupied only about half the total area. However, as can be seen from examples that were actually carried out, the forms are rather questionable. What looks good on paper often appears lifeless and stiff in reality.

In the formal gardens of the early years of this century, parterres did not fully regain their significance because the focus was now on flower borders with their wonderful arrangement of herbaceous plants. It was not until the 1930s and in the period after World War II that garden designers again produced genuine parterre designs. Vita Sackville-West adopted fully the idea of box edging and in the White Garden at Sissinghurst Castle all the beds are bordered in the old-fashioned way with box. Geoffrey Jellicoe created a traditional box parterre in 1934 in

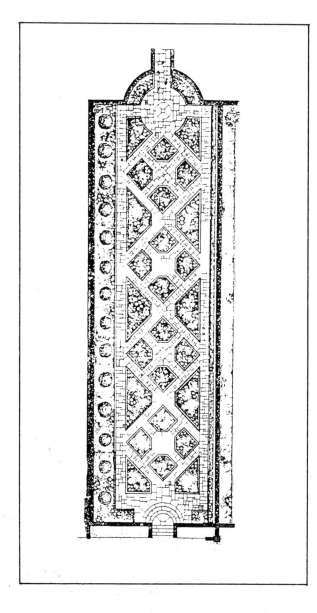

Ditchley Park near Oxford, and Russell Page also produced many new variations on the theme. In his gardens in Switzerland and in France he planted parterres with box and grey-leaved artemisia. For Longleat, too, in 1951, he designed beautiful parterre strips. Finally, Norah Lindsay successfully combined the flower border with the traditional form of the parterre. At the beginning of the 1930s she designed a very successful one for Blickling Hall and in 1938 planned the parterre of Mottisfont Abbey (see Figs. 83 and 85).

One or two very remarkable parterre gardens have been created in recent years. In 1960 in the garden of Moseley Old Hall near Birmingham the National Trust laid out a parterre in the 17th-century style. In just a few years the low box hedges, gravel surfacing and privet clipped into ball shapes have produced a very convincing picture (Figs. 88 and 89). Parterres were also reconstructed in many other National Trust properties. In Little Moreton Hall in Cheshire a pretty parterre with box, lawn and gravel surfacing was laid out in the garden of a restored timber-framed house, to give it a more attractive setting. In Westbury Court in Gloucestershire a parterre has been reconstructed along the lines of a 17th-century model. Finally, another parterre worth seeing is that created in the early 1980s at Ham House in Richmond, near London, where box, lavender and artemisia present a very impressive picture. In Barnsley House (see pp. 208ff.) Rosemary Verey recently reconstructed a small knot garden. This bears a great resemblance to the woodcut in *Hypnerotomachia Poliphili* – and even now, 500 years after this work was published, the knot garden is still a very charming feature.

91   Ham House, Richmond, Surrey. The basic structure of
the parterre has remained largely the same since the 17th
century. As part of restoration work in 1975 the National
Trust decided on a simple planting scheme with squares
and triangles edged with dwarf box. The beds are planted
with lavender and santolina. This both corresponds to 17th-
century tastes and also fits in with current requirements in
that it is relatively easy to maintain.

The Sunken Garden

... Speak not – whisper not;
Here bloweth thyme and bergamot;
Dark-spiked rosemary and myrrh,
Lean-stalked, purple lavender.
WALTER DE LA MARE, 'THE SUNKEN GARDEN'[51]

The 'sunken garden' is a specifically English motif.
It can be described very easily: it is a generally
rectangular, not very large section of garden that is
80 to 120 centimetres (30 to 48 inches) lower than
the surrounding level. It is surrounded on all four
sides by small embankments or retaining walls
and has shallow steps leading down into it.

The design virtually dictates that it should have
a central focal point, generally a pond, a fountain,
a sundial or a small lawn. It is a clearly delineated
garden space, but without the kind of hard division
created by a hedge or a wall.

The motif of the sunken garden is a specifically
English form in garden design. There are examples of lowered garden sections in Renaissance
and Baroque gardens, such as the 4- to 5-metres
(13- to 16-ft) deep nymphaeums in the Villa Giulia
in Rome and the Zwinger in Dresden,[52] but these
are hardly related in terms of concept. A closer
comparison would be with the lowered garden
sections found in a few Baroque gardens, such as

92 Sunken gardens.
a) Packwood House, Warwickshire.
b) Marsh Court, Hampshire.
c) For comparison: Vienna, Belvedere Palace Garden, after
an engraving dated 1737.
d) Country house near Biggar, Borders Region, Scotland.
e) For comparison: Vienna, Belvedere Palace Garden, after
an engraving dated 1737.
f) Packwood House, Lapworth in Warwickshire.
g) Marsh Court, Hampshire.
h) Happisburgh, Norfolk, designed by C.E. Mallows, 1908.
i) The Den, Cropthorn, Cheshire.

a

b

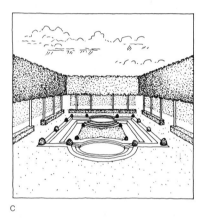
c

d

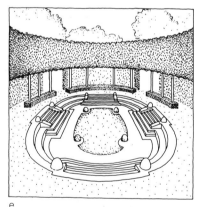
e

f

g

h

i

93 Packwood House, Lapworth in Warwickshire. This sunken garden is without doubt one of the most beautiful in England. The difference in height brings the flowers closer to eye level where their beauty can be even better appreciated.

that of the Belvedere Palace in Vienna (see Fig. 92e). However, here the designers were merely varying the relief in the garden; it did not develop into a separate theme as with the sunken gardens in England.

The motif of the sunken garden was already evident in garden design in England in the 17th century. In many engravings in *Britannia Illustrata* a number of sections can be clearly identified as specially designed sunken gardens. One of the gardens shown in Kip's engravings can also be seen in a contemporary painting (see Fig. 14), completed in 1680 by an unknown artist, which shows the garden of Pierrepont House in Nottinghamshire. In it we can see a parterre garden, 2 to 3 metres (6 to 10 ft) lower than the surrounding garden and enclosed on all sides by retaining walls. This painting suggests that one of the reasons for the development of the basic form of the sunken garden may have been the search for an adequate means of protection against the wind.

One of the oldest sunken gardens is that of Hampton Court. It is also variously described as a pond garden or a Dutch garden. This part of the palace gardens is thought to date from the time of Henry VIII, from the middle of the 16th century, but the first actual documentary evidence dates from the end of the 17th century, from an engraving in *Britannia Illustrata*.

This sunken garden doubtless served as a model for decades. Today, Hampton Court has a status similar to that of Versailles in France or the Villa d'Este in Italy. Its park and gardens also serve as recreation space for the metropolis of London.

The many visitors, however, are not allowed down into the sunken garden; they can only view it from above. The garden is, of course, very well tended, but nevertheless attracts some criticism. Its planting with the ubiquitous tagetes and red dwarf begonias creates a riot of colour, but is otherwise lacking in the highly developed sensitivity essential to well-coordinated planting schemes.

Nowhere in the specialist English literature is justice done to the sunken garden as a design motif. Reginald Blomfield and Inigo Thomas do mention the one at Hampton Court, but say nothing of its particular quality, or of its typological uniqueness. Likewise, in *The Art and Craft of Garden Making*, a comprehensive work published in 1900 by the architect Thomas Mawson, there is no thorough treatment of this design element. It appears that Edwin Lutyens was the first to rediscover it. In many of his designs created between 1901 and 1910, in particular those at Marsh Court, Folly Farm, Hestercombe House and Great Dixter, he included a sunken garden in the overall concept.

Astonishingly, the motif of the sunken garden, like none other in English garden design, was recognized as a special feature by garden designers abroad and adopted as a model.[53] In 1906 and again in 1910 the German journal *Die Gartenkunst* published an illustrated article on the sunken garden at Hampton Court.[54] In 1908 the journal *Die Woche* published a collection of competition designs for house gardens, one of the most interesting records of German garden design in the early 20th century; many of the designs made use of the motif of the sunken garden.[55]

A particularly successful design, for example, is the one by the Stuttgart architect, Adolf Mössinger.[56] His design for a garden near Heilbronn appeared under an English-language motto in a clear reference to English garden design.

Many variations on the theme of a sunken garden can also be found in the book *Haus und Garten*, published in 1914 and written by the architect and university professor, Friedrich Ostendorf,[57] and also in various articles in the journal *Die Gartenkunst*.[58] Clearly, the motif was quickly grasped and gratefully adopted as a suitable design tool in the spatial organization of gardens on a level site.

Karl Foerster, who is quite rightly regarded as this century's greatest German gardener and writer on gardens, also displayed a preference for pretty little sunken gardens, describing them as 'welcome showcases for selected groupings of herbaceous plants'. He also mentioned an aspect that would have been a particularly well-loved feature in many of the sunken gardens created around 1900 – plants growing from between paving slabs and out of stone walls.[59] Sunken gardens were particularly suitable in this respect. In England the practice was called wall gardening, and many suggestions for, and examples of, this feature appeared at the time in the relevant literature. Wall gardening presented on the one hand a tempting opportunity to supersede, or at least play down, the dictates of architecture, and, on the other, such locations proved to be ideal for many plants, especially for rockery perennials. The stones acted as a thermal store and there was no build-up of standing water.

94 Netherton House, near Biggar, Borders Region in Scotland. A slightly lower section in the lawn creates a distinct break and defines a separate area of the garden.

95 Packwood House, Lapworth in Warwickshire, created around 1930. Within the large lawn a smaller area is marked out by a yew hedge. Inside this area, a few steps down from the lawn, is a pond surrounded by glorious herbaceous borders.

96 Great Dixter House and Gardens, near Northiam in
East Sussex. Sir Edwin Lutyens designed this sunken
garden in around 1910.

Flower Borders and Colour Schemes

*I try for beauty and harmony everywhere, and
especially for harmony of colour.*
GERTRUDE JEKYLL, 1901[60]

*Fill up the flower-growing space with things that
are free and interesting in their growth, leaving
Nature to do the desired complexity, which she
will certainly not fail to do ...*
WILLIAM MORRIS[61]

Flower borders are the greatest innovation in the
iconography of the formal garden. They can be
divided into herbaceous borders, mixed borders
and shrub borders. The design intention behind all
these borders is best expressed in the mixed
border, which is planted mainly with herbaceous
plants, but supplemented with bulbs, annuals,
grasses, ferns, roses and decorative shrubs.
Pedigree has no significance in these uninhibited
arrangements. Wild plants generally regarded as
weeds can be found alongside carefully bred
varieties, plants with wonderful flowers next to
mediocre blooms that earn their place simply by
virtue of their beautiful leaves or interesting fruits.
The most important selection criteria are the individual plant's expressiveness and its contribution
to the overall harmony of the picture. English
borders, especially in the summer months, are

97 Flower borders at Bampton Manor between Witney
and Faringdon, Oxfordshire. Ground plan and section of the
facing plate.

98 Bampton Manor between Witney and Faringdon,
Oxfordshire. The planting scheme for these beds, designed
by Countess Munster, shows great sensitivity for colour.
The garden has now changed hands and the beds have
been narrowed to cut down on maintenance; the grand
effect has thus been diminished.

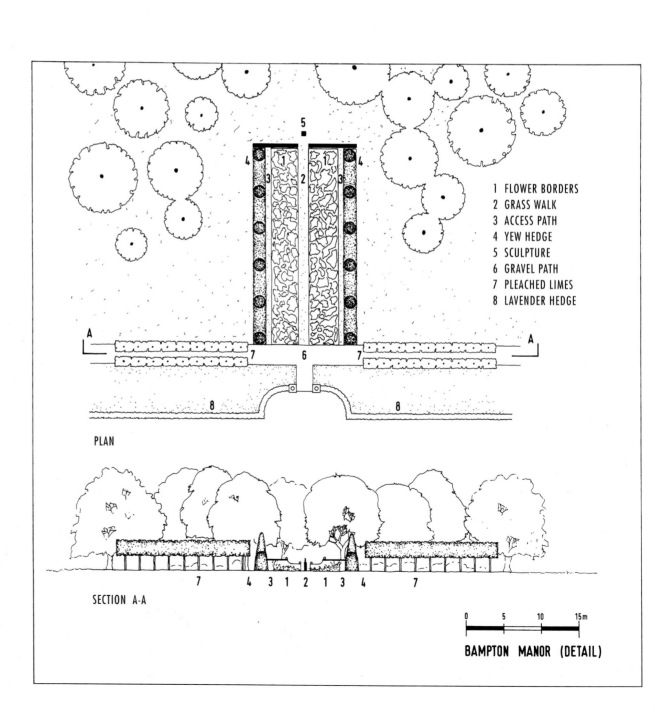

1 FLOWER BORDERS
2 GRASS WALK
3 ACCESS PATH
4 YEW HEDGE
5 SCULPTURE
6 GRAVEL PATH
7 PLEACHED LIMES
8 LAVENDER HEDGE

PLAN

SECTION A-A

BAMPTON MANOR (DETAIL)

intoxicatingly beautiful, but the photographer will soon discover that this great beauty and the carefully coordinated colour tones are virtually impossible to capture adequately on film.

It is obvious that a great deal of experience lies behind the design of these borders, both in terms of practical gardening ability and artistic and compositional skill. Planning a flower border demands a lot of knowledge about the type of soil and care and maintenance needed by each plant, and also about the different growth habits. When in flower many of the larger plants look rather unattractive lower down, and this must be disguised by a clever staggering of heights in the bed. The various flowering times must also be taken into account because the beauty and overall harmony of colour is intended to last continuously for several months.

A border is generally 3 to 6 metres (10 to 20 ft) wide and between 8 and 80 metres (25 and 250 ft) long. The width is especially important in successfully grouping the plants. Russell Page pointed out that most herbaceous plants are in fact meadow flowers and therefore best grown in generously sized beds.[62] At the back of the border is either a hedge or a wall, to protect the plants from the wind and also to provide a suitable background and frame for the composition.

The history of borders as an element in garden design began in the middle of the 19th century. In 1846 in the garden of Arley Hall, Rowland Egerton Warburton laid out an 80-metre (250-ft) long and about 5-metre (16-ft) wide double bed and filled it with flowering herbaceous plants. Similar beds soon appeared in the gardens of other country houses. Year after year, work would have continued on perfecting the overall picture. More and more types of plants and new cultivars were becoming available, and, thanks to the work of English painters, there was increasing appreciation of good composition.

Gertrude Jekyll is inseparably linked with the history of English flower borders. Her ideas were very influential and even today the guidelines she laid down are a model for garden design in the whole of Europe. She brought a painter's eye to gardening, thus enriching the formal garden by a precious new element of design.

In the 1930s Vita Sackville-West took up the mantle of Gertrude Jekyll and created compositions of great beauty. After World War II Christopher Lloyd made a name for himself in this field. And today, Penelope Hobhouse is generally regarded as the leading light. She has worked for the National Trust and from 1980–93 also looked after the garden of Tintinhull. But in many small private gardens, too, the owners and gardeners are constantly experimenting with new plant combinations.

One practice worth a special mention is the idea of planting borders with a particular colour theme. Some will have red tones only, some just blue, others perhaps all shades of yellow, or graduated shades of pink, lilac, mauve, violet and indigo. The most impressive colour-theme garden is the white garden, where a very special charm can be achieved through the renunciation of flower colour.

Even when the weather is dull and rainy white gardens have a surprising luminosity, and the range of tones from a warm creamy white to violet or pink-tinges is very impressive. With less emphasis on the colour of the flowers, the focus falls more on the shape. Then the endless shades of green and the variety of leaf shapes really come to the fore. Yellow-green, grey-green, silver-grey, variegated grey and white, shiny, felted, feathery, fleshy, matt, prickly, hard, soft, lanceolate, heart-shaped, rounded, hairy – all of this stands out.

The idea of arranging areas of the garden along colour lines is a concept that had already been tried out in architecture. In the Baroque architecture of the royal courts of Europe, single-colour themes were allocated to individual halls or rooms. At the end of the 19th century Gertrude Jekyll introduced this practice into garden design.

Similar ideas appeared surprisingly early in Germany. Josef Maria Olbrich, a leading Jugendstil architect, designed colour-theme gardens for exhibition at the Regional Show in Darmstadt. All that remains of these are one or two watercolour sketches and some contemporary photographs.[63] Although the designs themselves appear to be very effective, the photographs show that they did not transfer successfully into actual gardens, which look pitifully stiff, with no sign of luxuriant vegetation. Clearly, the architect just did not have the necessary knowledge of gardening, which is quite a different skill and one that can only be fully mastered after years of practical experience. The main reason why the designs of Gertrude Jekyll and Edwin Lutyens were so successful lies in the fact that both were grand masters of their art.

The idea of flower borders was adopted throughout Europe. However, it must be said that on the Continent these borders never seem to equal the perfection reached in England, despite the availability of a wide range of herbaceous plants. One of the reasons is certainly the incorrect assumption that all that is needed for success is a lot of willing hands. Well-tended beds need well-trained gardeners who have a feeling for their work. Herbaceous borders only appear to be firmly established, permanent features, whereas in fact they need constant shaping and encouragement from a gardener if they are to carry on looking as they should.

99 Watercolour by George Elgood. The picture was created in 1901 as an illustration for Gertrude Jekyll's work *Some English Gardens.* It shows the aster beds at Munstead Wood, Gertrude Jekyll's country house.

101 Hole Park, Rolvenden, near Cranbrook in Kent. This
border, backed by high yew hedges, is planted in shades
of yellow and white.

Topiary Work

*If the apple be pruned for its purpose of fruitage,
why not the yew for its purpose of shapeliness?*
EDWARD PRIOR, 1901 [64]

The word topiary is used to describe the decorative clipped forms of trees and shrubs, mostly yew and box, sometimes also ilex, juniper or hornbeam. The word itself comes from the Latin expression *opus topiarium*. In Ancient Greece and Rome artistically clipped forms were a popular type of garden ornament. In Renaissance gardens, too, they were a favourite feature. In his richly illustrated novel *Hypnerotomachia Poliphili*, published at the end of the 15th century,[65] the Italian Francesco Colonna describes highly unusual and complicated shapes created by clipping trees and shrubs. This work had a major influence in other countries, and clipped forms were soon eagerly imitated throughout Europe. In England, topiary was already common in the Tudor period of the first half of the 16th century. It is likely that the idea had been taken from Dutch garden design, which, in turn, was influenced by Italian Renaissance gardens and in particular by their clipped work. At the end of the 17th century, topiary work reached extremes, with gardeners producing ever more daring shapes. It seems as

102 Topiary.
a) Peckover House, Cambridgeshire.
b) Levens Hall, Cumbria.
c) Bradfield House, Devon.
d) Knightshayes Court, Devon.
e) Tintinhull House Garden, Somerset.
f) Tapeley Park, Devon.
g) The Orchard Farm in Broadway, Hereford and Worcestershire.
h) White Garden of Hidcote Manor Garden, Gloucestershire.
i) Lytes Cary Manor, Somerset.

a

b

c

d

e

f

g

h

i

103 Earlshall Castle Gardens in Leuchars near St Andrews in the Fife Region, Scotland. This 16th-century castle was renovated in 1890 by the architect Sir Robert Lorimer. During this time the topiary garden was started. In its simplicity and clarity it is one of the most beautiful examples of the art.

104 Small private garden in Broadway in Hereford and Worcestershire. In the Cotswolds, one of the most beautiful parts of England, one finds many such examples of clipped yew and box, not only in the larger country-house gardens but also in small cottage gardens.

105 Athelhampton House Gardens, near Puddletown in Dorset. This garden was designed by Inigo Thomas in 1893, along strictly classical lines. The yew pyramids have grown into grandiose green sculptures.

if gardening ambitions were focused solely on creating and maintaining artistically clipped trees and shrubs.

When, in the 18th century, the landscape garden became the ideal in garden design, topiary work came under fierce criticism. It was the focus of the landscapists' attack on the formal style and the object of sharp ridicule.

As the landscape style gradually began to usurp the position of the formal garden, many of the larger country-house gardens began to lose their topiary. Yet not everyone was willing to do away with work that had taken decades of painstaking shaping. In smaller gardens, in particular, the topiary work did not fall victim to the fashion for the landscape garden, and this also remained true in the 18th and 19th centuries.

In her writings at the end of the 19th and at the beginning of the 20th century, Gertrude Jekyll was still able to state that there were many examples of topiary art in old gardens, and her photos proved it.[66] She maintained that topiary should not be overdone, but considered it a legitimate feature of garden design. A whole chapter of *Garden Ornament*[67] is devoted to this subject, citing many remarkable examples.

In around 1900, with renewed interest in formal gardens, topiary enjoyed a wave of rehabilitation. Geometric and non-figurative forms were preferred to figurative ones, and among the latter only the bird motif was tolerated. Reginald Blomfield, writing in 1892, stated that, when used correctly, topiary can lend a very picturesque quality to a garden.[68] In their books *Formal Gardens in England and Scotland*[69] and *The Art and Craft of Garden Making*,[70] published in 1902 and 1900 respectively, Inigo Triggs and Thomas Mawson presented extensive examples of, and pattern sheets for, topiary work. The figures are mostly combinations of cubes and cylinders, and all look as if they could have come straight from a turner's lathe.

Interestingly, the magazine *Country Life*, which, around 1900, was a great advocate of the formal garden, had a topiary motif in its colophon: the shape of a peacock cut out of yew.

Topiary work is also very effective in winter, as it presents a constant shape, changing little with the seasons.

Even today, heated debate surrounds the practice of clipping trees and bushes. Condemnation as mere kitsch, and accusations of 'a rape of nature' fall easily from some lips. Yet these judgements are too hasty. Writing in *The Studio* in 1901 Edward Prior gave the definitive answer to the question of justification for topiary: 'The answer is complete to those who complain of the clipping of a tree in a garden as a "perversion of Nature". If you cut grass, because, when so cut, Nature gives it growth, a neatness and an order which man thinks fitting, why not for the same end cut your trees and shrubs? If paths are to be kept and beds to be weeded, why must not trees be shaped and trimmed? If the apple be pruned for its purpose of fruitage, why not the yew for its purpose of shapeliness?'[71] One can only support this argument: Nevertheless, it does not clear allay all misgivings. Even Francis Bacon put pen to paper on the subject. He found clipped work in architectural and sculptural forms pleasing, but criticized figurative topiary as fit only for children.[72]

There is another criterion for appraisal: surely the only important point is the question of how, where and in what context topiary is used? If it serves the overall concept, then figurative topiary can be justified. When, for example, two bird figures cut out of yew are used to frame a gateway like green sculptures, and if this is appropriate in its context, then it is both a legitimate and original stylistic device in garden design.

Topiary gardens, in which are grouped many different sculptural shapes, can also be very effective and impressive. The most famous topiary gardens are at Levens Hall in Cumbria and Packwood House in Warwickshire. Both gardens date from the 17th century and have remained almost unchanged since that time. As both are surrounded by lush countryside, the contrast with domesticated nature in the form of topiary is particularly charming. Another aspect that should be mentioned is that in England, for example in the Cotswolds, topiary work has a long and very popular tradition. Clipped shapes of yew and box can be found in both the gardens of the larger country houses and in those of many smaller cottages.

It is difficult to imagine topiary work, especially figurative shapes, being widely adopted in modern garden design. Although contemporary designers would welcome the use of topiary in sculptural and geometric forms there is nowadays no time for them to grow, since new gardens generally have to present a more or less complete picture within the space of just a few months, while a piece of topiary may take decades to reach its final form.

106 Small private garden in Weston Subedge near Broadway in Gloucestershire. The most common form of figurative topiary are birds, such as peacocks and hens.

107 Kennel Holt near Cranbrook in Kent. Yew hedges with topiary decoration frame the drive and entrance to this country house.

Statuary

Even in Ancient Greece and Rome gardens were adorned with statuary. During the Italian Renaissance the use of garden sculpture reached a peak, and in the 17th and 18th centuries the tradition was continued by French artists. No independent development in garden statuary can be traced in England; practice here was guided instead by tastes on the Continent. In the landscape garden sculptural decoration lost its significance. Only in the late 19th century did interest in this form of ornament reawaken. In the revival of the formal style of garden, sculpture was also rediscovered as a useful stylistic element.

Among the various types of sculpture in a formal garden, both non-figurative examples, in the form of obelisks, balls or stone vases, are found as well as figurative ones. As in Italian Renaissance gardens the motifs were derived from classical imagery. We find representations

a

b

c

d

e

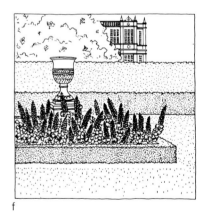
f

g

h

i

108 Statuary.
a) Jenkyn Place, Hampshire.
b) Tyningham, East Lothian, Scotland.
c) Anglesey Abbey, Cambridgeshire.
d) Madresfield Court, Hereford and Worcestershire.
e) The Postern, Kent.
f) Longleat, Wiltshire.
g) Brockenhurst Park, Hampshire.
h) The Green, Cumbria.
i) Chatsworth, Derbyshire.

109 Pusey House Gardens, near Faringdon in Oxfordshire. The walls around the large garden terrace were built in 1935 to plans by Sir Geoffrey Jellicoe. In true classical style marble busts are placed in sculpture niches in the walls.

110 Anglesey Abbey, Lode in Cambridgeshire. The most common non-figurative sculptures are obelisks, balls and above all stone urns or vases. They are often placed at the end of an alley or a garden path, or they are used to mark the centre of a bed or area of garden.

111 Misarden Park Gardens, near Stroud in Gloucestershire. This ensemble of sculpture, yew hedge and lady's mantle (*Alchemilla mollis*) has great beauty.

112 Knightshayes Court, near Tiverton in Devon. The moss-covered sandstone sculpture is placed in the centre of a circular bed planted with catmint (*Nepeta fassenii*).

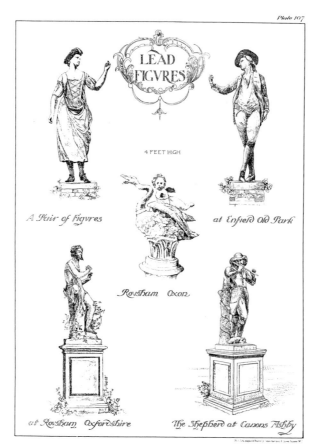

113, 114 The plates are taken from *Formal Gardens in England and Scotland*, written by Inigo Triggs and published in 1902.

of ancient gods, such as Diana, goddess of the hunt, with her dogs, or Ceres, goddess of the harvest, carrying great sheaves of corn, and a merry Bacchus, god of wine, with the goat-legged Pan. The most common deity, of course, is Flora, the goddess of flowers, carrying a cornucopia overflowing with blossom. Garden gates or entrances to individual sections of the garden are often guarded by sphinxes or lions. Some biblical representations can also be found, such as Cain and Abel, or David and Goliath. Another favourite motif is the putto: the boy cupid with bow and arrow. The allegory of the Four Seasons, depicted as four different putti, is a very charming theme. Even in Ancient Greece and Rome these sturdy little figures were symbols of fertility and love.[75] Pastoral motifs, such as a flute-playing shepherd or pairs of a country lad and his lass were also very popular.

At the beginning of the 20th century some sculptors tried to extend the repertoire of sculptures to include representations of animals and birds such as owls, parrots, cats, tortoises and squirrels.[76] Although these works displayed great skill they never rivalled classical motifs in popularity.

The most common non-figurative motifs are obelisks, balls and stone urns or vases. The pref-erence for vessel-shaped statuary is particularly noticeable. Generally, these vases are carved out of solid stone or are of hollow-cast metal. Many have rich relief decoration in the form of garlands of flowers or scenes such as found on Greek vases, with ornaments, putti heads or similar. Vases are one of the earliest cult and art objects; they are an archetypal symbol of life itself, and particularly of the female life-force, of the woman and mother. This symbolic significance has lost much of its strength in this day and age, but nevertheless a number of painters and sculptors in the 20th century have used this metaphor, especially in *Jugendstil* art and Symbolism.[77]

In English gardens sundials are a predominant element. They were not only an established part of the design repertoire in gardens of the late 19th and early 20th centuries, but were also a firm feature of gardens in the Middle Ages, the Renaissance and the 17th century. Sundials are specially made for their particular location in line with the complicated laws of astronomy govern-ing the angle of the gnomon or pointer. Generally, they are made entirely of bronze and placed on an artistically shaped, richly ornamented baluster column, or are supported by a figure. The place-ment of the sundial in the overall plan of the garden is always of great significance; it can be at the intersection of two paths, or in the middle of a parterre or knot garden. Its importance is further underlined by placing the whole sundial and column on a stepped pedestal. In earlier centuries, of course, the sundial was popular for its genuinely practical function of telling the time, but in the gardens of the 19th and 20th centuries this played a very small role. Despite the fact that a well-designed and correctly set up sundial can tell the time accurately to within only about five minutes, it really is no more than a toy, given today's technology. Nevertheless, the great charm of sundials is beyond doubt. Alwin Seifert, a garden designer from Munich, summed this up very aptly in an article that appeared in 1932 in the German magazine, *Gartenkunst*, where he described them as 'witnesses and indicators of the iron laws which bind us to the cosmos'.

Sandstone is a very suitable material for garden statues. In the English climate it soon takes on an attractive grey patina with lichen and moss. It grows into its environment and once more becomes a piece of nature. Marble, on the other hand, is not so suitable as it simply blackens but does not develop any patina. Also, it always looks rather out of place in England, as it needs the

115, 116 Urns and vases, sundials and lead sculptures are among the most popular types of ornamentation in formal gardens in England. Around 1900 there was a thriving, highly skilled industry involved in the manufacture of these garden accessories.

warmth and luminosity of the southern skies to be fully appreciated.

Lead is a particularly attractive material, especially in English weather and light conditions. In fact, most English garden sculptures are made of lead. The first foundries put in an appearance in the middle of the 17th century, and by the 18th century leadwork was in great favour for garden sculpture and architectural decoration. Experience in working lead to produce medals and plaques was developed over many centuries and the manufacturing processes for this metal were much cheaper and simpler than for bronze. With a minimum of effort it was possible to produce large numbers of copies of classical sculptures or replicas of Italian Renaissance motifs.

Eighteenth-century London had many large lead foundries and workshops, the most famous being owned by a Dutchman, Jan van Nost, whose range of garden statuary was the widest and most beautiful. It seems, however, that people did not immediately take to the material. Lead sculptures were often coated with sand to make them look like sandstone, or covered with oil paints, often even entirely gilded.[78] Today we find lead sculptures undoubtedly most pleasing when they are left natural, especially as they

develop a very attractive silver-grey patina in the English climate. Like bronze, lead is also unaffected by the weather. The only disadvantage of this soft material is that it is exceptionally vulnerable to wilful damage: its surface can be scratched easily with a fingernail.

Just as interesting as the sculptures themselves and the materials from which they are made is the way they are integrated into the overall garden scheme. Often statuary is used in connection with the architectural elements of the garden – the terrace, balustrade, steps, gateway and the space-defining hedges. Generally, it is also sited where it will draw the eye, or as the end marker of an alley or a garden path. Alternatively, a statue may form the focal point of a bed or a particular area of garden, or be framed by a hedge laid out in a semicircle around it. Some sculptures are placed in wall niches.

Even quite modestly sized pieces of sculpture can set up an effective contrast and enhance our appreciation of the charms of nature. For it is without doubt the proximity of a light-coloured stone vase or a silver-grey lead sculpture that really brings out the wonderful dark green of a yew hedge.

In a few gardens created after World War II, an attempt was made to include modern sculptures

in the overall design. One such was Geoffrey Jellicoe's design for the garden at Sutton Place. Certainly, placing modern sculptures outside in natural settings can enhance them, and indeed some of the most renowned British sculptors from Henry Moore to Ian Hamilton Finlay knew how to use the interaction between nature and sculpture to show off their work to best effect. Nevertheless, with very few exceptions, the general impression is that the old, classical style of sculpture fits best into a garden setting.

Is this just because we are accustomed to this type of sculpture or might it perhaps have something to do with the fact that today's sculptors have different aims to those of garden designers? Are they no longer prepared to have their sculptures serve simply as an integral part of a larger work of art?

Francis Bacon's criticism, quoted at the beginning of this chapter, in which he questioned the value and purpose of statuary as garden ornament, is certainly too sweeping. And to Hermann Muthesius's note we must add that the placement of statuary demands great sensitivity. A garden sculpture can only unfold its charms when integrated into the overall scheme to form a single, harmonious design.

THE ENGLISH FORMAL GARDEN – STATUARY

117 Hazelby Garden, near Newbury in Berkshire. A country lad and his lass were favourite sculptural motifs in the 18th century. The sculptures are cast in lead and their grey tones create an effective contrast with the surrounding plants.

118 Hazelby Garden, near Newbury in Berkshire. Sundials are one of the most popular forms of garden ornament. In this example three lead-cast putti hold the dial aloft.

THE ENGLISH FORMAL GARDEN – STATUARY

119 Lead putto in the garden of Jenkyn Place, near Bentley in Hampshire.

120 Hazelby Garden, near Newbury in Berkshire. This 1.5-metres (5-ft) high lead figure is placed not far from her male counterpart.

Garden Seats

Here let peace and contentment reign
Inscription on a garden seat, c.1905 [79]

The seats in English gardens are of such impressive quality and beauty that they deserve a separate chapter. It is not without good reason that they are considered here immediately after the chapter on garden statuary, because garden seats can often be as charming and effective as a piece of sculpture.

Until recently garden seats were generally made of oak, but today teak is normally used. Teak has great resistance to damp and it takes a very long time to rot. In view of these qualities, the wood is often left without any surface treatment whatsoever and within the space of a few months outside it will develop a very attractive silver-grey patina, just as oak does, and harmonize well with the colours of the surrounding vegetation.

For reasons of design, however, a contrast is often desirable, and a perfectly shaped garden seat lends itself very well to this purpose. The clearest contrast can be achieved with white,

121 Garden seats.
a) The Priory, Kemerton, Gloucestershire.
b) Felbrigg Hall, Norfolk.
c) Blickling Hall, Norfolk.
d) Greenwood, East Sussex, designed by Thomas Mawson in 1908.
e) Old Place, Sussex.
f) The Corbels, Cumbria, designed by Thomas Mawson in 1907.
g) In a small private garden in London.
h) Sissinghurst Castle Garden, Kent.
i) Hidcote Manor Garden, Gloucestershire.

122 Newby Hall and Gardens, near Ripon in North Yorkshire. The white-painted bench is positioned to form an effective ensemble with the wonderful copper beech, the yew hedge and the lawn.

a

b

c

d

e

f

g

h

i

which even today is the most popular choice for garden seats. A familiar sight in an English garden is the elegant picture of a classic white garden seat in front of a dark green yew hedge.

Perhaps garden designers in the past pursued the question of colour a little more thoroughly than nowadays, and used a wider range of tones than just white or natural. Gertrude Jekyll, who found white too dominant a colour, advised a grey 'like the colour of old weather-boarding or some very quiet tone of green'.[80] She also recommended painting all the wooden elements in the garden – gates, fences, plant containers, pergolas and garden seats – the same colour. Where this advice was followed, as in the garden of Snowshill Manor (see pp. 188ff.), we can see the sense and value in it, as it gives line and order to the whole garden.

From Kent to Scotland the same twelve or so types of garden seat can be found. Most of these styles have remained unchanged for many decades, which is an indication of a well-developed, mature design. They are also very solidly built examples of good craftsmanship and as such correspond fully to the ideals of the Arts and Crafts movement. One particularly interesting and unusual model for a garden seat was designed in around 1910 by Sir Edwin Lutyens (see Fig. 123). The back does not have the usual vertical slats, but horizontal ones, and the top is finished off with a wide elegantly curved frame. This distinctive contour is reminiscent of Biedermeier sofas. Lutyens's design can be regarded as one of the most refined seat models. Its effect can only

really be appreciated in an equally generously designed setting.

Other notable examples are one or two very elegant models with backs made of an unusual but attractive grid of diagonal slats (see Fig. 125). This style goes back to designs produced by William Chambers in the second half of the 18th century. Chambers was influenced here by the distinctive grid patterns in traditional Chinese carpentry.

In addition to garden seats made of wood, there are also examples in stone that were very popular at the turn of the century. Most were copies of Italian designs, and Gertrude Jekyll thought them to be unsurpassed and indispensable when the garden design has to conform to the style of a palatial building. At the same time she regretted, quite rightly, that stone seats are cold and uncomfortable.[81]

Sometimes metal seats can be found, mostly in cast iron and modelled in the Victorian style, which, for present tastes, is rather too intricate. Occasionally, graceful wrought-iron examples fashioned in the Regency style (see Fig. 124) can be seen.

However much we may admire the seats themselves, attention should be paid to the integration of these items of furniture into the overall design. In formal gardens, seats, like sculptures, are always part of a clear overall scheme. Their position is not arbitrary, but carefully considered and already designated in the basic plan as a seating area. A garden seat can be enclosed on three sides or in a semicircle by a hedge or wall, which shelters the back of the seat from wind and

creates a more intimate atmosphere. The idea of placing garden seats in wall niches had already been advocated in 1677 by John Worlidge in his work, *Systema Horticulturae or Art of Gardening*.[82] Worlidge also recommended placing a seat at the end of a garden walk and this is still common practice today. The intended location for the seat is marked out by a solid base of stone slabs, which gives both a firm foundation and prevents water collecting around the seat.

In view of the fact that in most years the climate of the British Isles grants only a limited number of hours of sunshine, and that the weather is seldom suitable for sitting outside, one might wonder why so much effort should be expended on designing garden seats, or why indeed seats are to be found in practically every area of the garden. It is, after all, not the Mediterranean, where people can sit out for many hours around stone tables under a pergola. English garden seats are designed more as a place to rest for a short while, and their main purpose is to enhance the picture of the garden. The seating ensemble, a reminder of happy hours spent there, is also arranged like a picture, full of the promise of future pleasures.

As people are apt to let their thoughts wander while resting on garden seats, these are a favourite location for inscriptions, as too are sundials. Mostly the inscriptions are epigrams of a general nature, such as that quoted at the beginning of this chapter, but in smaller private gardens they can be more personal, commemorating a family occasion, for example.

123 Sissinghurst Castle Garden, near Cranbrook in Kent. This design for a garden bench with elegantly curved back was created in 1910 by Sir Edwin Lutyens. A high brick wall clad with clematis forms a semicircle around the seat and creates an architectural space.

124 Hidcote Manor Garden in Gloucestershire. The graceful lines of this wrought-iron bench are reminiscent of the Regency style.

125 Chatsworth, Bakewell in Derbyshire. Here, too, the attractive picture derives not only from the design of the seat, but also from its integration into a clear overall scheme. In a formal garden seats are placed in positions that have been allocated as sitting areas in the design.

126 Bateman's, near Burwash, Etchingham in East Sussex. The semicircular garden seat is backed by a yew hedge.

Water

The pond has always been one of the most welcome design motifs in a garden ...
HERMANN MUTHESIUS, 1920 [83]

Water has always been one of the most important design elements in gardens. Old murals show that even the ancient Egyptians decorated their palace gardens with rectangular ponds. Ornamental pools also figured in Indian garden design, in Moorish gardens in Spain and in the European gardens in the Renaissance and the Baroque periods. In English formal gardens, the water generally features in the form of a pool or a pond.

Francis Bacon recommended that a pool should be 30 or 40 feet square, and free of fish, slime and mud. The water should not be allowed to stand to become green, mossy or foul smelling, but should be changed constantly. He even went so far as to advise, somewhat absurdly, that the basin be cleaned out once a day by hand.

Hermann Muthesius, the German architect, who was familiar with the English gardens being created at the turn of the century, drew up a set of

127 Pools.
a) Little Onn Hall, Staffordshire, designed in 1895 by Thomas Mawson.
b) Lennoxwood, near Windlesham, designed by Charles Edward Mallows.
c) Gledstone Hall, North Yorkshire, designed by Sir Edwin Lutyens.
d) Barrington Court, Somerset.
e) Athelhampton House Gardens, Dorset.
f) Hestercombe Gardens, Somerset. A round pond forms the focus of this walled garden.
g) Snowshill Manor, Gloucestershire.
h) Hestercombe Gardens, Somerset, designed by Sir Edwin Lutyens. A long, narrow water channel extends through the garden.
i) Abbotswood, near Stow-on-the-Wold, Gloucestershire, designed by Sir Edwin Lutyens 1901.

128 Folly Farm, Sulhamstead in Berkshire. The large, rectangular pond, created in 1901 to plans by Sir Edwin Lutyens, forms an attractive ensemble with the façade of the house.

129   Abbotswood, near Stow-on-the-Wold in Gloucestershire, designed in 1902. The water feature in the form of a grotto-like niche, seen here in combination with a rectangular lily pond, is a design motif often found in Sir Edwin Lutyens's gardens.

130   Cornwell Manor, near Chipping Norton in Oxfordshire. The pond is located directly on a water axis which starts at the entrance façade of the Manor and extends far out into the surrounding countryside.

131   Cornwell Manor, near Chipping Norton in Oxfordshire. The view of the house from the pond framed by weeping willows. The pond is constantly fed with fresh water from a stream running through the garden.

132–135 The drawings are taken from articles in *The Studio*. Between 1908 and 1910 the architect Charles Edward Mallows wrote and illustrated a series on 'Architectural Gardening'.

rules for designing a garden pond.[84] First of all he stipulated that it should have a regular shape. Pools with a clear geometric outline, known as shaped pools, are generally round or rectangular. Muthesius's second rule was that the pool should have a proper edge made of stone and that this edge should project only a little above the surrounding garden. In English gardens the pools tend to be surrounded by a carefully laid perimeter, usually 50 to 80 centimetres (20 to 30 in) wide and made of stone flags or rows of bricks. In most cases this paving is level with the surrounding lawn and the surface of the water is only a few centimetres below that. Unlike the Renaissance gardens, where pools were framed with stone balustrades, those in English gardens have no such spatial division, a circumstance that lends emphasis to the material contrast between the surface of the water and that of the lawn. The interplay of stone and water has an archetypal charm: the rigid, heavy, artificially shaped stone on the one hand and the transparent, moving image of the water on the other. Francis Bacon seems also to have been aware of this. He mentioned that stone paving around a pool always looks good. Muthesius's third rule stated that a pond should occupy an important spot in the garden, such as on the main axis, or that it should form the focal point of a part of the garden.

While in southern climates the charm of a pond derives from its reflection of the clear, bright sky, in England an important aspect is the decoration afforded by water lilies. The best effect is achieved when about a quarter of the total surface area is covered with these plants. The stone, the quiet water with its light reflections and the pale flowers on glossy green leaves floating on dark water make a charming picture. We are reminded of Claude Monet, for whom the water lilies on his garden

pond in Giverny became the most important motif of his life's work. In his paintings the water lily became the very symbol of life, of *joie de vivre* and of form unfolding from dark, formless depths.

Walled, stone-edged pools or tanks are not the only form of pond found in English garden design: there are also large, rectangular fish-ponds with a grass bank surround instead of a stone edge. Francis Bacon found these unacceptable as an element of garden design, writing, in his essay on gardens: '... but Pools mar all, and make the Garden unwholesome, and full of Flies and Frogs.' Reginald Blomfield and Inigo Thomas, however, considered them to be an important feature and praised fish ponds for their beauty

and for their practical value as a means of providing fish for the table.

Elaborate water pieces are seldom found in English gardens. For Francis Bacon fountains were 'a great Beauty and Refreshment',[85] and for Inigo Triggs they were the 'most delightful garden decoration'.[86] Both authors probably had Italian or French gardens in mind and failed to realize that in the English climate fountains can never have the same kind of charm as they have in Southern Europe. Although there were water pieces in the more ostentatious gardens of the 16th and 17th centuries,[87] these features have little significance in the formal garden of the 20th century. The few small water spouts or water-spouting sculptures that can

be found are mostly replicas of Italian models.

The architect Edwin Lutyens added one or two very attractive examples to the repertoire of designs with water. He was influenced, it seems, both by the water axes in Italian Renaissance gardens, such as that of the Villa Lante, and by the gardens of the East, above all those of Kashmir. In Renaissance gardens the idea of the linear water axis, laid out as a series of cascades, constituted a key integrating element in the overall design, and Lutyens took up this idea but substituted an equally deep, but narrow, 30-centimetre (12-inch) wide, walled channel, or rill, planted with lilies. This motif can be found again and again in his garden designs.

136 Howick Gardens, near Alnwick, Northumberland. A circular pond reflecting the sky forms a calm central focus for the whole garden design. A special feature of this garden is its long flower beds planted entirely with blue agapanthus.

137, 138 Knightshayes Court, near Tiverton in Devon. A lily pond forms the central point of this splendid area of garden bounded by perfect yew hedges.

Lawns and Flower Meadows

An 'English lawn' is synonymous with a perfect expanse of grass. Nowhere else in Europe can lawns of such amazing perfection be found. The English lawn is even, dense, fresh and velvety, almost like a fabric. And the edges are cut so precisely that it is hard to imagine how it is possible, let alone how such sharp lines can be maintained.[89]

The secret of these perfect lawns lies in the painstaking care and effort lavished upon them by English gardeners – plus, of course, the benefits of a good deal of experience. First the soil must be thoroughly prepared before planting the seed. Care should be taken to provide adequate drainage and a good even surface, as well as to make sure that soil type and grass seed are suited. Later, when the grass is established, it must be regularly cut, rolled and finally fertilized, if the aim of a perfect lawn is to be achieved.

In recent years the rise of the 'ecological garden' has led to the English lawn becoming a target of criticism, because it is thought that such perfection can only be achieved with the help of herbicides. Without wishing to denigrate the 'ecological garden', which indeed has its own place and context, it must be said that the English lawn also has a role within a corresponding

overall concept. A perfect lawn is also sometimes disparaged as an expression of misplaced and exaggerated fussiness, which indeed it is, when, as seen in some smaller gardens, a gardener channels all his energies into producing a weed-free, closely mown lawn. A garden that consists only of a lawn speaks of a great lack of imagination. In the formal garden, however, the lawn is one element within an over-all concept and it is an indispensable design tool.

Were it not for the invention of the lawn mower in 1830 the English lawn would be unimaginable. It is well to remember that before that time the only implements available for cutting grass were scythes and shears. The lawn mower was invented by Edwin Budding, an engineer. He adapted a technique used in the manufacture of velvet and needlecord, whereby the

139 Cricket. Pen drawing by Heywood Summer, c.1895. The game is played on a level expanse of grass. In the 19th century many new games emerged for playing on grass. Croquet was also very popular and even today in English country houses it is generally possible to find the appropriate equipment for playing this game. And, as the name suggests, lawn tennis is also played on grass courts.

140 Clifford Chambers, near Stratford-upon-Avon in Warwickshire. These perfect lawns act as a handsome surround for the skilfully proportioned façade of a country house renovated by Sir Edwin Lutyens in 1921.

141 Jenkyn Place in Bentley in Hampshire. At the edge of the terrace adjoining the house begins an almost 300-metre long stretch of lawn. Angled slightly towards the building, it has an unusual charm.

142 This small country-house garden near Lechlade in Oxfordshire shows an attractive combination of lawn and flower meadow.

143 Hardwick Hall, near Chesterfield in Derbyshire. Intersecting hedge-lined paths dissect the garden into four zones. The grass walks are like fine carpeting and lead to a distinct focal point, here a garden seat and a splendid tree.

loops in the cloth were trimmed to produce an even pile. Budding's lawn mower had cutting blades arranged in a spiral pattern around a rotating cylinder. It was relatively easy to use and the cut it achieved was much more even than that possible by hand. Within a short space of time many different models of lawn mower came on the market. Even today, some quality-conscious gardeners prefer Budding's cylinder mower to the later invention of scythe-type mowers with horizontally rotating blades. The cylinder mower gives a finer cut and for days afterwards it is possible to see the mown 'stripes' formed by the reflecting light, like damask cloth. This effect is particularly prized by those in search of the perfect lawn.

If the word 'hedge' conjures up an impression of three-dimensional space, then the word 'lawn' suggests a flat plane. We perceive level, homogeneous expanses to be calming. John Dando Sedding, the Arts and Crafts architect, thought lawns were 'a vision of peace and a source of unutterable value'.[90] Without doubt, an open expanse is pleasing to the human eye; it gives a point of reference and contrast amidst the variety of the garden.

In the formal garden the lawn, as a design element, generally features as a wide expanse in front of the house, below the terrace. It gives an unobstructed view from the house and presents a horizon around which is arranged the surrounding vegetation and topography. From the garden, it offers an unobstructed view of the house and thus enables the latter's architectural composition to be seen to best advantage.

Another practice is to create a 'green room' by enclosing the lawn with hedges. This juxtaposition of a level expanse with the vertical element of the hedge creates the impression of an architectural space. Often such spaces are used for various lawn games or as a place to sit.

In addition to such 'introverted' expanses of lawn there are also linear, hedge-lined grass walks, some of which can be several hundred metres long, reaching out to a distant focal point. Here, too, the spatial design is understood only through the relationship with the perfect flat plane of the grass. Alternatively such grass walks are flanked on both sides by herbaceous borders. Here again the combination of a flat plane with the vertical element of the plants brings out the composition of the borders. If the borders can be said to be composed like a painting, then the adjoining lawn supplies the necessary frame, transforming the whole design into a picture.

English garden design not only has the lawn, it also has the meadow, generally laid out under fruit trees. In spring such meadows unfold their full splendour. Snowdrops, crocuses, narcissi, scilla, bluebells, daffodils and tulips turn it into a sea of blossom. When the bulbs have died down they are left untouched until June. The grass grows high and the bulbs gather strength before the meadow is cut again.

Literary sources and old paintings show that lawns were already employed as elements of garden design in the Middle Ages. However, a closer inspection of these sources reveals not so much a lawn as we know it, but more of a flower meadow. In both literature and painting there are many references to the variety of plants in these 'lawns'.

In the 16th century we find representations[91] of small lawns which are not yet comparable with the English lawn we know today, but neither are they exactly flower meadows. The enthusiasm for a colourful carpet of flowers seems to have given way to a desire for a uniform, closely cropped, level expanse of grass. Sources reveal that these lawns were also used as areas for sitting, for which purpose short grass lent itself much better than a luxuriant flower meadow.

By now another aspect was becoming important, as evidenced by numerous engravings and paintings: from as early as the 16th century onwards lawns were being used for the playing of various ball games. Here, again, short grass was preferable. About half of the 80 engravings of country houses in *Britannia Illustrata*, published in 1707, depict a lawn on which people are playing bowls, a game which in England, unlike its French counterpart boules, is always played on grass. The lawn on which bowls is played is called a bowling green, and this term has now become synonymous in garden design with a wide expanse of level, closely mown grass.

Summerhouses

The formal garden is incomplete without a summerhouse.
THOMAS MAWSON, 1900 [92]

In all epochs of garden design summerhouses or garden pavilions have played an important role. The Italian-style garden of the Manor House in Llanerch in Denbighshire, Wales (see Fig. 13) has a garden pavilion, which is also very Italian in siting and design. Garden pavilions were a key element in the overall composition of both Italian Renaissance gardens and English gardens of the 17th century.

Even in the 18th century the significance of summerhouses did not decline. On the contrary, they developed into exquisitely worked constructions, small classical-style temples or Chinese pagodas. Their main function was to draw the eye and to be noticed from a distance. Thus they were more like objects to be viewed than a building for actual use.

In the formal garden of the 20th century the summerhouse again plays a role more like that of the pavilions of 17th-century gardens. As is clear from the quote by Thomas Mawson, above, they have an important formal function. As a distinctive compositional element they clarify and

144 Summerhouses.
a) Montacute House, Somerset.
b) Wych Cross Place, Sussex.
c) Hidcote Manor Garden, Gloucestershire.
d) The Green, Cumbria.
e) Stonyhurst College, Lancashire.
f) Water pavilion and boathouse at Kearsney, Kent.
g) Great Maytham Hall, near Rolvenden in Kent, designed by Sir Edwin Lutyens in 1910.
h) Ionic temple in Hall Barn Garden, Buckinghamshire.
i) Peover Hall, Cheshire.

a

b

c

d

e

f

g

h

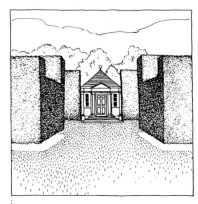
i

145 Hazelby Garden, near Newbury in Berkshire. This pretty summerhouse was built quite recently. It is intended less as a place to sit and more as a work of art, an eye-catching feature and trellis for the climbing roses.

146 Eyford House, near Upper Slaughter in Gloucestershire. This little tea house, just 10 metres (33 ft) away from the main house, was constructed in the 1960s, but its design is carefully harmonized with that of the house, built in 1910.

147 Hidcote Manor Garden, near Chipping Campden in Gloucestershire. The two identical pavilions with their curved roofs, red brickwork and white mullioned windows have become the symbol of this garden not only for their distinctive, beautifully proportioned form, but also for their skilful placement in the overall design.

emphasize the formal structure of the overall design of the garden.

A summerhouse can mark the end of a path, as in Hidcote Manor (see p. 139 and p. 177). Or, it can act as a vertical element at the end of a long horizontal, like a terrace, as seen, for example, in the garden of Parnham House (see p. 161). Typical, too, is placement on the inside corners of perimeter walls. As many old engravings and paintings show this was quite common in formal gardens of the 17th century (see Fig. 12). In the formal garden of the 20th century this design idea was again taken up. Despite the delicate appearance of many pavilions they have a very distinctive effect, marking out the corners of the garden and the sphere of influence of the house.

Generally, great attention is paid to the design of summerhouses, and many have very precise detailing. The basic structure and the design of the façades is always clear and simple. In plan they are mostly rectangular and they generally have a pyramidal roof. Stone or brick is used for the walls. In around 1900 wooden garden pavilions with delicate trelliswork were popular, although nowadays these are quite rare. Wooden constructions are not particularly long-lasting especially if the material is not treated adequately.

As already mentioned, garden pavilions were a favourite device for gardeners of the formal style. It seems almost as if their practical function was secondary, especially in view of the fact that a garden may well have had several such pavilions.

The most important reason for building a summerhouse is to provide a protected place to sit outside in natural surroundings. While in Italy garden pavilions were a welcome shelter from the heat, in English gardens they more often provide refuge from the ever-recurring rain showers and the wind. Nevertheless, temperatures often permit a short spell in the garden, and even in dull or rainy weather, the summerhouse is a pleasant spot to sit after lunch or in which to serve afternoon tea. In the 17th century summerhouses were sometimes called banqueting houses; the name indicates that people didn't just gather together in them on mild summer evenings, but that they also dined here.

Often it seems as if architects sought to justify the presence of a summerhouse as a functional building. Thomas Mawson, for example, suggested setting one up as a children's playhouse. He also recommended using it as a small library for books about gardens and nature. In garden designs of around 1900, we often find summerhouses designated as fishing lodges, if they are sited by the water, or as bowling pavilions, if alongside a large lawn. In other instances the summerhouse is described as an apple store, a cool, airy place to store the apple harvest. The dovecote is another favourite element in the formal garden.

Gertrude Jekyll stated that a summerhouse should be comfortable and practical.[93] She saw it as a place to keep games and cushioned seating; it should be capable of holding all the garden furniture. The garden tools and other appliances were generally kept in a simple shed, sited in a less prominent position.

When designing a summerhouse it must be remembered that it is only pleasant to sit in when well built and maintained. As it is not used for more than half the year, the danger is that it will be neglected. Each spring it must be thoroughly cleared of dust and cobwebs. One wonders indeed why such great attention is paid to this little place in the garden. Perhaps the answer is to be found under the shady plane trees in the famous Renaissance garden of Villa Lante. Here, to the right and left of a natural spring emerging from a moss-clad rock face, are two stone pavilions, which in the 16th century were already known as *loggie delle muse*. This name indicates something that is very important for creative people: in a summerhouse one feels nearer to the muses. Medieval illustrations even depict poets composing their works in the garden[94] or monks deep in religious meditation.[95] Goethe wrote in his garden house in Weimar; Franz Liszt composed in the garden of the Villa d'Este; Claude Monet, Emil Nolde and many other painters had their studio in the garden.

The themes of young lovers and lovers' trysts in secluded spots in the garden are found again and again in poetry and painting. Rudolf Borchardt accurately described the background to this phenomenon in 1928: 'Man is torn between lost nature and an unattainable god-creator. A garden is at the very centre of this tension. This is the most fundamental reason why man dreams of his origins in a garden, and why he seeks to find transfiguration, redemption and comfort in gardens. This is also why he instinctively loves gardens and devotes himself to them...'[96]

shire. The summerhouse, placed at the end of a path
bordered by beautiful herbaceous borders, is the focal point
of this part of the garden.

The Kitchen Garden

I have always thought a kitchen garden a more pleasant sight than the finest orangery, or artificial greenhouse.
JOSEPH ADDISON, 1712 [97]

The kitchen garden also features in the overall scheme of a formal garden. Remarkably, it is the part of the garden that has changed least since the Middle Ages. The kitchen garden today, like those depicted in the medieval woodcuts from *Britannia Illustrata*, is still a walled garden. The walls and, in some cases, the hedges give the necessary protection against the wind. For purely practical reasons kitchen gardens, along with outbuildings, greenhouses and working quarters, also figured in the gardens of country houses in the 18th century. Thus even during the heyday of the landscapists one element of an older garden style remained; hidden behind high walls this little-regarded part of the garden still had its admirers. In 1712 Joseph Addison, the statesman and writer, wrote in the *Spectator*, 'I love to see everything in its perfection: and am more pleased to survey my rows of coleworths [carrots] and cabbages, with a thousand nameless pot-herbs, springing up in their full fragrancy and verdure, than to see the tender plants of foreign countries kept alive by artificial heats, or withering in an air and soil that are not adapted to them'.[98]

For reasons of pure practicality, a kitchen garden is set out in a clear, logical arrangement. As a rule it is divided into four equal sections by intersecting paths. Often, the main paths are lined with espalier-trained fruit trees, which is a very traditional custom, as shown by engravings from the 17th century. In *The Gardener's Dictionary*, published in 1733, we read: 'The four sections of the kitchen garden are usually bordered by espalier-trained fruit trees. When correctly planted and carefully tended, they produce an effect which is unequalled by even the most beautiful parterre and the most perfect pleasure garden. What could be more beautiful than to walk between tidy hedges of fruit trees, full of wonderful blossom in spring and in late summer decorated with beautiful fruit. The espalier-trained fruit trees also protect the gardener working on the beds from unwelcome attention and from the vagaries of the weather.'

Within, the sections narrow, and beaten paths mark out strips of long rectangular beds. Everything here is well ordered with herbs, lettuce, vegetables and fruit bushes generally planted in rows. The support frames for beans and peas and the wires for raspberries and blackberries are also, of course, linear constructions. Everything shares the same logical order and arrangement. This structure is overlaid with a wonderful variety of vegetables, such as large-leaved rhubarb, feathery-topped carrots, the wonderful blue-green and grey-green cabbage varieties, the sturdy-leaved leeks and the bizarrely shaped leaves of the artichoke. There is great charm, too, in the blossom of the pea and bean plants, in the umbels of dill and in the large golden yellow flowers of the courgette. Here is Molly Keane, writing about the kitchen garden: 'The sun shone alike upon Lady Bird and Miss Parker within the shelter of the kitchen garden. The late fruit blossom was trained rosy and trim, against the walls, the early cabbages throve, the peas and the beans throve, also the spring onions, the lettuces and every other class and kind of vegetable that was grown there. The subdued regularity of their squares and lines and patches was solid and pleasing and as it should be.'[99]

It is after all in the kitchen garden that our sense of smell is stimulated more than in any other part of the garden. One only has to think of a freshly cut bunch of chervil or parsley, of basil, rosemary, sage, marjoram, dill, mint or the wonderfully exotic scent of nipped-off tomato shoots.

Generally, an English kitchen garden also contains some decorative plants, such as roses, various shrubs, dahlias, a bed of annuals or a trellis with sweet peas, grown mainly for cut flowers. Even in gardens of the Middle Ages we can see evidence of this uninhibited combination of decorative plants and vegetables. In Renaissance and Baroque gardens, vegetables played no part whatsoever in garden design. Yet behind the walls of English kitchen gardens they remained in colourful co-existence for many centuries. In the 18th century, in the era of the landscape garden when flowers were banished, the kitchen garden was the sole refuge for all flowering plants. In the 19th century the beds of flowers in the kitchen garden were discovered by painters and finally became an inspiration for the flower border, which was introduced as an important structural element in the formal garden.

In England, kitchen gardens often retain their traditional charm. Many country-house hotels take pride in pointing out that the vegetables served at table were grown in the hotel's own kitchen garden. Some of the National Trust properties also have kitchen gardens that are still tended. Visitors can buy fruit and vegetables, or pay a small sum to pick their own fruit.

149 Barnsley House, near Cirencester in Gloucestershire. A carefully laid out and tended kitchen garden with its wonderful variety of plants is a real match for any arrangement of purely decorative plants.

Orchards

Orchards are even more personal in their charms than gardens, as they are more nearly human creations. Ornaments of the homestead, they subordinate other features of it; and such is their sway over the landscape that house and owner appear accidents without them
AMOS BRONSON ALCOTT [100]

To the English the word 'orchard' means more than just a garden of fruit trees – it conjures up a little of the charm and imagery of paradise. Many village pubs proudly bear the name The Orchard. Country hotels that have an orchard as well as a garden and croquet lawn know how to exploit this in their advertising.

Woodcuts, book illustrations and contemporary texts show that fruit trees were an established part of gardens from the Middle Ages through into the 16th and 17th centuries. A description from 1575 of the garden at Kenilworth tells of areas of the garden decorated with exquisite obelisks and planted with apple, pear and cherry trees.[101] For Francis Bacon, too, it was quite natural to combine fruit trees, decorative plants and garden ornamentation. He saw not the least necessity to distinguish between the beauty of fruit trees and plants that served a purely decorative purpose. The blossom of the apple, peach, cherry and plum

150 Drawing by Max Graumüller, 1908. Fruit trees, too, can be used to create a very impressive garden.

151 The edge of Porlock village in Somerset; pen drawing by Mary L. Newill, *c.* 1895. In England orchards create a smooth transition between the village and the open countryside.

152 Penns in the Rocks, near Groombridge in Sussex. The blossom of fruit trees is surely one of the most attractive sights a garden has to offer.

153 Cornwell Manor, near Chipping Norton in Oxfordshire. Fruit trees form the basic design framework in this kitchen garden and orchard.

154 Pitmedden Garden, near Udny in the Grampian Region of Scotland. Orchards in Scotland and in England are often enclosed with walls to protect the trees against the wind. An ancient tradition, reaching back to the Middle Ages, is to train fruit trees against the orchard walls.

trees were for him on a par with that of lilac and lavender, or of roses, violets or honeysuckle.[102]

In *The New Orchard and Garden*, published in 1618, William Lawson sings the praises of the orchard: 'What more can your eye want to see, or your ear to hear, your mouth to taste, or your nose to smell, that is not all here in its most perfect beauty in an orchard?'[103]

Developments in garden design in Continental Europe, where fruit trees were no longer acceptable in late Renaissance or Baroque gardens meant that these trees also began to lose their place in the English garden. For the English landscape gardens of the 18th and 19th centuries they were unthinkable. Fruit trees were regarded as having unattractive trunks and dull-coloured blossom; they were also thought to be too reminiscent of working life.

Nevertheless, for purely practical reasons, landscape gardens in the 18th century did have walled areas for fruit trees and bushes, but these never formed part of the overall design, nor was any effort expended on their artistic or aesthetic arrangement.

It was not until the second half of the 19th century that voices were again raised in defence of orchards. This newly awakened appreciation of fruit trees in blossom first found expression in painting. Orchards were a favourite subject for artists in Victorian England. One of the most beautiful examples is the 1859 painting by John Everett Millais, entitled simply *The Orchard*.[104] This picture of young girls gathered under blossoming fruit trees is England's response to Botticelli's *Primavera*. Botticelli's collection of gods and demigods among tall orange trees is translated by the Pre-Raphaelite Millais into a lifelike group of young girls under apple blossom. Millais's painting also seeks to show that an ordinary apple tree in its full spring glory is in no way inferior to the orange grove in Botticelli's work.

In 1892 Reginald Blomfield and Inigo Thomas set out their plea for the orchard from the point of view of the garden designer, but not without launching a hefty sideswipe at the advocates of the landscape style: 'Nothing can be more beautiful than some of the walks under the apple-trees in the gardens at Penshurst. Yet the landscape gardener would shudder at the idea of planting a grove or hedge of apple-trees in his garden. Instead of this he will give you a conifer or a monkey-puzzle...'[105]

Thomas Mawson also supported the practice of including an orchard in the formal garden in his book, *The Art and Craft of Garden Making*, published in 1900. For him among the greatest pleasures of the orchard were the bees it attracted at blossom time and the large numbers of birds to be found there at all times of the year. The joy in seeing birds in the orchard has a long tradition. Many medieval and early Renaissance paintings express this connection between garden trees and birds.[106] Even in the 18th century, in the heyday of the landscape garden, people recognized the pleasure of seeing and hearing birds in the orchard. In 1712 Joseph Addison wrote in the *Spectator*, 'I value my garden more for being full of blackbirds than cherries, and very frankly give them fruit for their songs.'[107]

Gertrude Jekyll was also a firm supporter of the orchard and even advocated that it be sited centrally in the garden, and not in the less important perimeter locations.[108]

She appreciated the orchard not merely for its fruit trees, but because it was an ideal location for many spring flowers, and she suggested planting masses of cowslips, snowdrops, narcissi, bluebells and other bulbs there. This idea is still very popular today, and anyone visiting England in April will be struck by the flower-filled meadows under a sea of fruit-tree blossom. As any gardener knows, bulbs are at their best in a meadow setting, where the conditions are also better suited to their growth habit than in a flower bed. The overall picture of the orchard is not the least spoiled if the meadow is left uncut for a few weeks or even months after the bulbs have finished flowering. During this time the bulbs can die back, undisturbed, and gather strength in time for the following year's display.

In the formal garden of the 20th century the orchard has once again become an important and established part of the overall design of a country-house garden. Apart from changing perceptions, another reason for its renewed popularity may perhaps be the increasing desire for self-sufficiency in fruit and vegetables.

The English
Formal Garden

Ten
Outstanding
Examples

Montacute House
An Elizabethan Garden in Somerset

Montacute House, four miles west of Yeovil, is one of the best preserved Elizabethan mansions in England. The garden, too, has retained much of its 16th- and 17th-century origins. Inside, the house bears the dates 1598 and 1599 and carved above the east door is the date of 1601, which probably marks the year of its completion. The house was built by Sir Edward Phelips, a successful lawyer who in 1611 became Master of the Rolls. He was also an influential politician and one of the most powerful men in the kingdom.

Montacute House was owned by the Phelips family for more than 300 years, and, in honour of their famous ancestor, the eldest sons were all christened Edward. In 1834 Montacute House passed to a collateral line, and in 1845 William and Ellen Phelips took up residence. The new occupants had a well-developed sense of style and a gardener with a good understanding of design, and together they made a number of changes to the garden. Many of the splendid trees we can admire today were planted at that time and, to the northwest of the main house, an orangery was built in the classicist style. For the last 30 years of his life, William Phelips (1823–89) was ill and the family finances declined drastically. His son, William Robert Phelips (1846–1919), was forced to sell off little by little the contents of the house and parts of the land. Finally, his heir, Gerard Almarus Phelips (1884–1940) had no alternative but to offer the property for sale. In 1931 the Society for the Protection of Ancient Buildings acquired the house and presented it in the same year to the National Trust. The house was newly

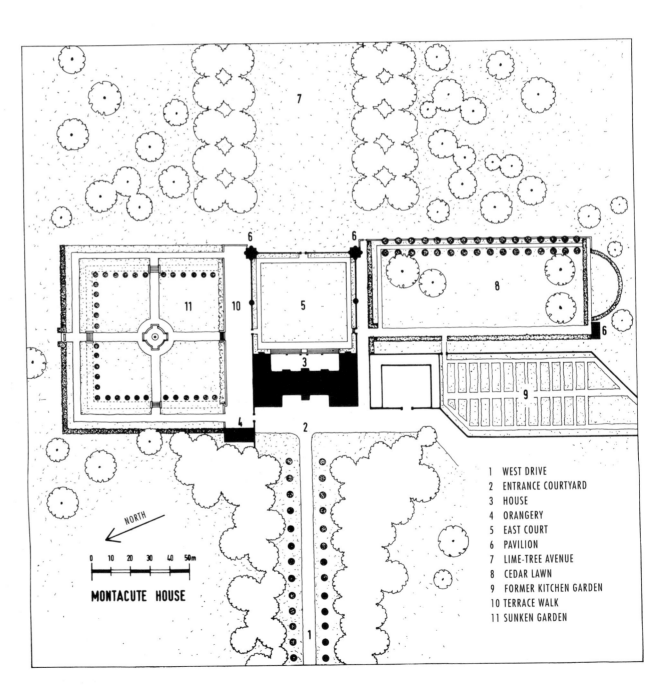

NORTH

0 10 20 30 40 50m

MONTACUTE HOUSE

1 WEST DRIVE
2 ENTRANCE COURTYARD
3 HOUSE
4 ORANGERY
5 EAST COURT
6 PAVILION
7 LIME-TREE AVENUE
8 CEDAR LAWN
9 FORMER KITCHEN GARDEN
10 TERRACE WALK
11 SUNKEN GARDEN

155 General plan of Montacute House and Garden in Somerset.

furnished with the help of numerous loans and gifts, and paintings were brought here from the Victoria and Albert Museum and the National Portrait Gallery.

In many respects Montacute House is a remarkably beautiful building. Its elegant proportions, light-filled rooms, the warm, golden-ochre colour of the sandstone walls, the ornate roof edge with obelisks, balustrade, decorative chimneys and beautifully curved Flemish-style gables all combine to create a wonderfully harmonious picture. This architectural masterpiece is attributed to William Arnold (d. 1637), who also designed Cranborne Manor in Dorset, Wadham College in Oxford and Dunster Castle in Somerset.

The fifth Edward Phelips (1725–97) enlarged the house in 1786–87 by adding an extension to the west side of the H-shaped building. For this he used whole sections of the façade and many decorative masonry details from a nearby house, Clifton Maybank, which was being partly demolished. This new façade, like that of Montacute carved from the local Ham Hill stone, formed the centre of a new main entrance, transferring it from the east to the west side. This unusual and difficult project was very successfully completed, and, it seems, without the help of an architect, just a few hard-working local builders. At least, no architect was mentioned in Edward Phelips's autobiographical notes. A new drive was also laid down in 1851, leading from the road to the house. Today this approach, the West Drive, is bordered by splendid mature

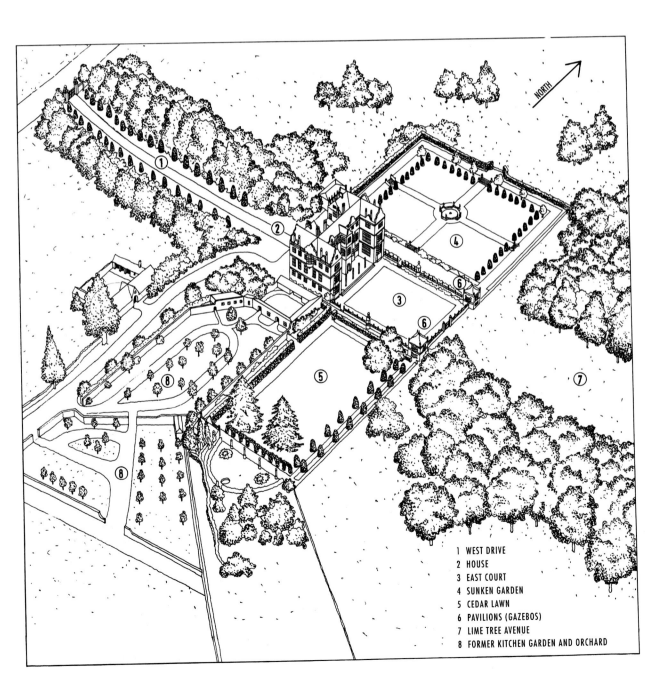

1 WEST DRIVE
2 HOUSE
3 EAST COURT
4 SUNKEN GARDEN
5 CEDAR LAWN
6 PAVILIONS (GAZEBOS)
7 LIME TREE AVENUE
8 FORMER KITCHEN GARDEN AND ORCHARD

157 Isometric projection of the garden of Montacute House. Redrawn from an illustration by the National Trust.

trees, grass verges and fronted by Irish yews clipped into cone shapes.

The drive is not used as a visitors' entrance, but walking down it one gets a splendid view of the house, especially in the late afternoon light. Visitors enter the grounds from the south, at the place where a 1782 plan marked the orchard and kitchen garden. The high walls now surrounding the car park once enclosed the kitchen garden. It seems rather a pity to have to approach the house from the side and along small paths, as this makes it more difficult to appreciate the overall composition.

The first part of the garden visitors enter is the Cedar Lawn, a large rectangular lawn bordered on the west by a stately yew hedge. The hedge is clipped into unusual soft curves, but is still very effective as an architectural, space-defining element. On the east of the Cedar Lawn is a double row of columnar yews, and on the south side, the two mighty old cedar trees that give the lawn its name. Most visitors pass on from here, without much further investigation, to the next part of the garden, the East Court, close to the house. This large area, once the actual forecourt to the house, measures 45 by 45 metres (150 by 150 ft) and is bordered on one side by the east façade of the house and on the other three sides by a perimeter wall, 1½ metres (5 ft) high. The balustrading and obelisks decorating the top of this wall blend very well with the architecture of the house. In two corners of the East Court are exquisitely designed pavilions, or gazebos, which complement the style of house and enhance the overall composition.

In front of the perimeter wall, on all three sides of the East Court, are wide mixed borders, a 20th-century addition, laid out in the 1930s to planting schemes drawn up by Phyllis Reiss.

(From 1933–53 Mrs Reiss created the garden at nearby Tintinhull – see p. 100 and Figs. 73 and 102 – which she gave to the National Trust in 1953.) Vita Sackville-West also advised on the planting of the flower borders. She decided upon strong colour schemes, selecting plants with leaves and flowers in warm oranges or golden yellows to harmonize with the characteristic honey-coloured stone, and purple, violet and indigo tones to complement it.

In front of the borders are wide gravel paths that run around the edges of the square lawn. An open space creates a calm point of reference and sets off the fine architecture to good effect. At one time there seems to have been a pond in the centre of the lawn, as shown on a sketch by Reginald Blomfield dated 1889.[109]

A gatehouse once stood between the two pavilions, but in 1787, when the fifth Edward Phelips moved the main entrance to the west side, it was replaced by a simple, large garden gate. Nowadays this gate is always kept closed, but the visitor can look through it into the surrounding parkland. A better view can be had from the windows in the upper floors of the house; from here one's gaze is drawn into the distance along an axis bordered right and left by double rows of enormous lime trees. Sheep and cattle graze between and among the rows of trees, creating a pastoral scene very fitting to this grand old English country house. Some visitors might find this close proximity of fine architecture and rural life a little surprising, but as evidenced in the engravings in *Britannia Illustrata*, it is a combination with a tradition reaching back hundreds of years. The sight of grazing cattle, herds of deer and flocks of sheep has long been prized for its restful qualities.

This wide axis with parkland is to be under-

stood not so much as a part of the surrounding landscape, but more as a key compositional element in the whole complex of house and garden. The architectural order and influence of the house reaches far out into the landscape and thus links the architecture to that landscape. We can see from a general plan, dated 1782, that coaches, riders and those travelling on foot would have approached the old gatehouse from the side, but the wide, tree-lined axis would almost certainly have been the point from which the lords of Montacute started out on their rides into the countryside, especially when hunting.

On the north side of the building is a part of the garden that is no less beautiful than the East Court. Its simple, clear lines are fully in keeping with the ideals of Elizabethan garden design. Regularly spaced clipped yews and a wide path, raised by about a metre and a half (5 ft), border an almost square, fine English lawn divided into four equal parts by paths that cross in the middle. The centre point is accentuated by a pond with a serpentine balustrade around it. The design of the pond is reminiscent of the Italian style and therefore quite appropriate to Elizabethan tastes, although it was not actually constructed until the 1890s. This was formerly the site of an Elizabethan high circular mount, or *Mons Acutus*. The present design of this northern part of the garden forms a perfect complement to the building, and it is hard to see how it could be improved. Those familiar with the structural components of the formal garden in England will recognize that this is in fact a sunken garden.

In the opinion of Reginald Blomfield and Inigo Thomas, Montacute House was one of the greatest achievements of English garden design, a view that we can still fully endorse today.

153

158   A wide axis, bordered on both sides by double rows of mature lime trees, leads off into the distance.

159, 160   The area of garden on the north façade of the house is divided into four quarters by two paths crossing in the middle. At the centre is a pond with a balustrade around it. Rows of clipped yews accentuate the spatial design and create an ensemble of simple grandeur and balance.

161   At the corners of the walls around the East Court are two exquisitely designed Elizabethan pavilions.

Parnham House
A Garden in the Spirit of Reginald Blomfield and Inigo Thomas

Parnham House is near the small town of Beaminster in the west of Dorset. The gently rolling countryside in this area is particularly beautiful, with small patches of woodland interspersed with meadows and fields. The approach to Parnham is through a wooded valley that gives way to parkland closer to the house.

The history of Parnham dates back to the 15th century. It was during this time that the Great Hall, the heart of the house, was built. In the 16th century the square-plan building was extended into an E-shape, in the style of Elizabethan manor houses. In the 19th century this clear layout was broken up by extensions built on the west and north sides. However, as the same golden-yellow sandstone was used, and the new sections were stylistically in keeping with the existing structure, a harmonious picture was preserved. Until the middle of the 18th century Parnham was in the hands of one family, and the house was the focal point of a large, flourishing estate. Through a change of owners in the early 19th century, this situation changed and the house became instead simply a grand country house. John Nash (1752–1835), the celebrated architect, whose style was very adaptable, was commissioned to design the new extensions in 1810. Dr Hans Sauer, who owned the house in the early 20th century, had the whole house restored and the gardens redesigned between 1910 and 1913. In the 1920s Parnham House was an exclusive country club, but in 1930, following financial problems, the receivers were called in. In the years that followed the house was used for various purposes. During World War II it served as a military hospital and

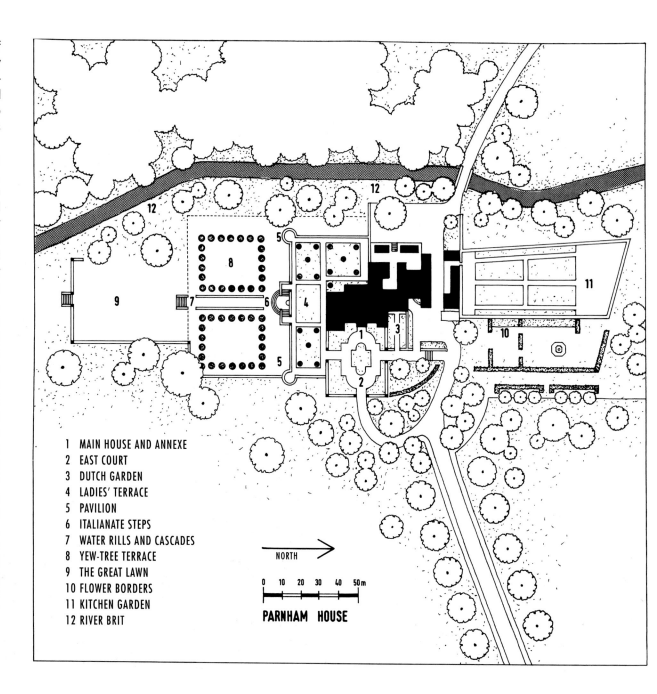

1 MAIN HOUSE AND ANNEXE
2 EAST COURT
3 DUTCH GARDEN
4 LADIES' TERRACE
5 PAVILION
6 ITALIANATE STEPS
7 WATER RILLS AND CASCADES
8 YEW-TREE TERRACE
9 THE GREAT LAWN
10 FLOWER BORDERS
11 KITCHEN GARDEN
12 RIVER BRIT

NORTH

0 10 20 30 40 50m

PARNHAM HOUSE

162 General plan of Parnham House in Dorset.

163 The entrance courtyard was the first part to be redesigned by Inigo Thomas between 1910 and 1913. The architect based his design on traditional styles.

subsequently, for almost 20 years, as an old people's home. The enforcement of fire regulations led to its closure in 1973 and it remained empty for three years until a new owner was found.

In 1976 Parnham House was acquired by the furniture designer John Makepeace. He saw this wonderful, historic house as an ideal location in which to realize his ambition to find a place where he could live as well as have enough room to set up his workshops and the seminar and exhibition space for a design centre.

The garden had been totally neglected and needed to be completely restored. It was not until the beginning of the 1980s that it emerged in its present form. Today the house, which is a Grade 1 listed building, and the gardens are open to visitors on two days a week.

There is no record of how the gardens originally looked. The design we see today is based largely on the redesign carried out between 1910 and 1913 by the architect Inigo Thomas (1866–1950), who also designed the gardens at Athelhampton (1891) and Chantmarle (1910) in Dorset and at Barrow Court (1892)[110] in Somerset (see p. 223). Inigo Thomas, co-author of the book *The Formal Garden in England*, published in 1892, is probably rather unjustifiably overshadowed by the better-known Blomfield. When their joint work appeared Thomas was 26 years old and Blomfield 36. As a young man, Inigo Thomas had acquired a wide knowledge of garden design, and had travelled much on the Continent. Even before the book appeared he had completed several gardens that were far more convincing as examples of the formal style than any of Blomfield's, and we can therefore assume that Thomas would indeed have had great influence on the text content of the book.

At the end of the 19th century Italian gardens were attracting a great deal of attention in England, and so, in 1893, Inigo Thomas set off on an extended tour of Italy. He visited the villas in Rome and Frascati and made many sketches there. He seems to have been particularly impressed by the Villa Lante in Bagnaia and the Palazzina Farnese in Caprarola,[111] but was also drawn to the kind of English garden seen at Montacute House, which itself had many parallels with Italian design.

The first part of the redesign of the garden in 1910 affected the East Court. Here, at the former main entrance to the house, Inigo Thomas laid out a courtyard with areas of lawn and gravel, bordered by a sandstone wall decorated with balustrading, obelisks and corner posts. This gave the house a fitting and traditional forecourt, in the style of 17th-century manor houses, such as can be seen in the engravings in *Britannia Illustrata*. The main purpose of a forecourt was to provide a suitable space for a carriage and horses to draw up and turn round. Although this is of course nowadays no longer a consideration, the area is still very important in terms of the overall design. It creates an inviting prelude to the house and a setting for the well-proportioned Elizabethan entrance façade. In addition, as the visitor enters the forecourt, he emerges from the shade of spreading, mature trees into the open courtyard, as if coming across a clearing in the woods. This impression is enhanced by the house's thickly wooded surroundings.

On the south side of the building Inigo Thomas created the Ladies' Terrace, measuring 15 metres (50 ft) wide by almost 100 metres (330 ft) long.

With its elegant balustrade, ceremonial, Italianate steps and two circular stone pavilions at each end, this terrace is indeed the most impressive design feature in the garden. Topographical factors tend to suggest that there was always a terrace at this point, although the present form is that designed by Inigo Thomas at the beginning of the 20th century. The main attraction of the Ladies' Terrace is its view down onto the second terrace, the Yew Tree Terrace. Here, on a wide, level expanse of lawn, are 50 shaped yews, clipped into cones, creating a picture that sets up an ideal counterpoint to the mature woodland of the surrounding landscape garden. This contrast between geometrically and mathematically ordered nature on the one hand and free-growing nature on the other is demonstrated here as one of the most effective stylistic tools in garden design. When walking through this part of the garden, the visitor is rewarded with ever-changing perspectives arising from the interplay of the cone-shaped yews and the splendid mature trees in the background. Also, the regular rows of yew bushes create visual lines of reference and enhance the sense of spatial depth.

The Yew Tree Terrace has a strictly axial design, with the main axis leading on into a third level of the garden, the Great Lawn, bordered at its southern edge by a pond. This axis is underlined by two narrow water rills running between the yew bushes and fed by water emerging from lions' heads at the Italianate steps. The water flows along the rills and down cascades by the steps to the Great Lawn. From there it continues underground into the lake. This water feature was reinstated in 1987.

To the north of the manor house, beyond the annexes, is a large, now unused, kitchen garden, surrounded by brick walls. Once espalier peaches grew against the south-facing walls here, and, as frost protection for these sensitive trees, fireplaces and chimneys were incorporated into the wall as a means of warming it.

A few years ago an 'Italian' garden was constructed to the east of the kitchen garden, where the bowling green used to be. However, there seems to be no real justification for the name, except perhaps for the fountain in the middle of the lawn. In fact this part would hardly be worth a visit, were it not for the very skilfully laid-out border along the back of the kitchen garden wall. At either end of the border is a high yew hedge, and a smaller hedge divides it into two sections. The first section is planted in colours of cool pinks, blues and violets, while the second has flowers in warm yellows, oranges and reds.

The most important parts of the garden of Parnham House are without doubt those designed by Inigo Thomas. He made this garden into one of the most beautiful examples of the formal garden revival in the early 20th century. Parnham House shows how the classical elements of garden design can be used to create a clear structure, which, although simple, can produce a magical effect. In comparison to the garden of Hidcote Manor (see p. 174), which was created at about the same time, and by a contemporary of Inigo Thomas, Lawrence Johnston (1871–1958), we can see that Parnham House is much more eclectic in design and lacks the innovative strength of Hidcote. However, in terms of sheer beauty, there is little to choose between them.

165 On the south side of the house Inigo Thomas created the Ladies' Terrace, 15 metres (50 ft) wide and almost 100 metres (330 ft) long. With its elegant balustrading and two circular pavilions at each end, it is one of the most impressive design features in the garden.

166 View of the south façade of the house from the lower terrace with its 50 clipped yews.

167 The steps leading down from the Ladies' Terrace to the Yew Tree Terrace were built in 1912, as part of a general redesign of the garden by Inigo Thomas.

Pitmedden

A Scottish Garden in the Style of the 17th Century

The impressive, wide-open landscape of the Highlands and the turreted, rough-stone castles of Scotland are not the only sights worth seeing north of the border – there are also many beautiful gardens. The National Trust for Scotland has more than 100 historic buildings, most of which merit a visit for their gardens alone.

Large parts of the south and east of Scotland do not look very different to the green hilly landscapes of Cornwall, Devon or Dorset. Typical features are fields of corn and pasture, divided up by hedges or lines of trees, and occasionally interspersed with small clumps of larch or Scots-pine woodland.

About 25 kilometres (15½ miles) north of Aberdeen is the garden of Pitmedden, which must be one of the most impressive properties owned by the National Trust for Scotland. An inscription above the garden gate states that the garden was created in 1675 by Sir Alexander Seton. His father, John Seton, from one of the oldest families in Aberdeenshire, had acquired Pitmedden in 1603, the memorable year in which the crowns of Scotland and England were joined, with the accession to the throne of James Stuart, the Sixth of Scotland and First of England.

There is no firm evidence of who designed the garden at Pitmedden, but it is known that Alexander Seton had connections with the excellent Scottish architect, Sir William Bruce of Balcaskie (1630–1710). Bruce had travelled in Holland and France and visited the garden of Vaux-le-Vicomte, designed in around 1650 by Le Nôtre. Bruce was responsible for the design of many country houses and gardens in Scotland, including

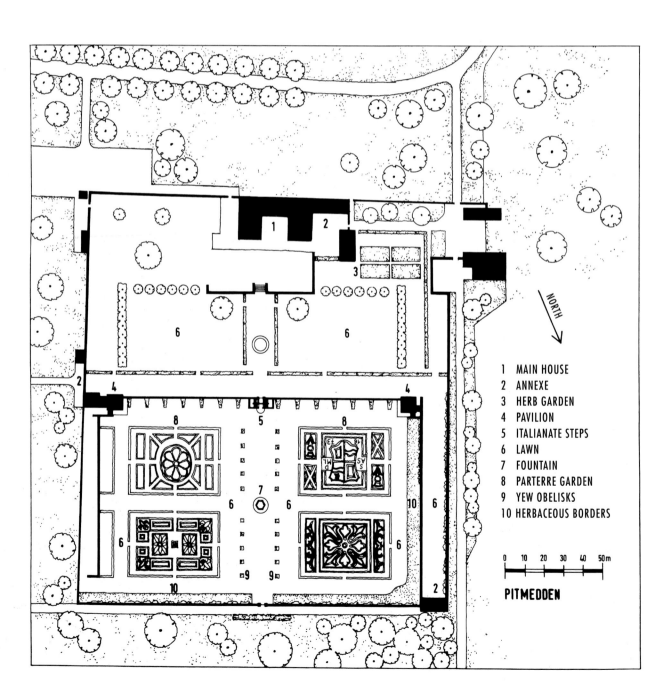

1 MAIN HOUSE
2 ANNEXE
3 HERB GARDEN
4 PAVILION
5 ITALIANATE STEPS
6 LAWN
7 FOUNTAIN
8 PARTERRE GARDEN
9 YEW OBELISKS
10 HERBACEOUS BORDERS

PITMEDDEN

168 General plan of Pitmedden, north of Aberdeen in Scotland

169 The parterre garden of Pitmedden is without doubt one of the most beautiful in the whole of Europe. It was created in 1952 as part of the reconstruction of this 300-year-old garden.

that of his own house, Kinross, near Edinburgh (see p. 225).

The garden may have no particular features pointing specifically to Bruce as its architect-creator, but its well-balanced proportions and carefully planned details do indicate a very skilful designer. For this reason Bruce is generally assumed to have had a hand in the design of Pitmedden.

In 1818 the house was badly damaged in a fire, and Pitmedden garden lost what was probably its most important compositional element. The house's papers also fell victim to the flames and with them any historic evidence there might have been of how the garden used to look. In 1860 most of the old house was replaced by a new Victorian-style building. This is the house we see today – a building that is inappropriate to the garden and which, in terms of design, has too little formal distinction. A more classical, grander house would seem more fitting.

In 1894 Pitmedden was acquired by a noted farmer, Alexander Keith. On the site of today's parterre he laid out a kitchen garden with espalier fruit trees against the high walls. The house passed to his son, who in 1952, a year before his death, gave Pitmedden to the National Trust for Scotland.

In 1952 the Trust began restoring the garden, which had been badly neglected during World War II. However, the basic structure and the architectural components, such as the walls, pavilions and the very well-proportioned Italianate garden steps were all in good condition.

The restoration works were headed by the antiquarian and former Inspector of Ancient Monuments in Scotland, Dr James S. Richardson. In the centre of the garden, where Alexander Keith had constructed his kitchen garden, a parterre was laid out. This corresponded more closely to the original design of the garden. In laying out this parterre inspiration was taken from James Gordon's 'bird's eye views'. This collection of maps of aerial views of the city of Edinburgh, is the most important document on Scottish garden design in the 17th century. Three of the four parterre sections were probably modelled directly on the bed designs for the Palace of Holyroodhouse in Edinburgh, as depicted in one of the engravings. The fourth parterre section is a new design, based on the coat-of-arms of the Seton family. The beds of annuals, with their box edging, are very skilfully designed and perfectly tended. Their glowing colours have great charm in the northern Scottish light and under the turbulent, often leaden skies. A very restful impression is created by placing the colourful beds against the fresh green of grass borders, instead of gravel paths.

The central axis consists of a broad strip of lawn almost 25 metres (80 ft) wide. This leads from the lower garden gate, past a hexagonal-shaped fountain in the middle of the parterre, through to the Italianate steps. Flanking the sides of this axis are yews clipped into obelisk shapes. Although the trees are of only modest height, at just 2.5 metres (8 ft), their precise, regular arrangement makes them a very expressive, aligning element in this part of the garden. In relief as well as spatial design the parterre garden is very effective. This derives on the one hand from the skilful proportioning of all elements and on the other from the fact that this section, too, is a walled garden. The walls are green with espalier apple trees growing against them. Herbaceous borders of about 4 metres (13 ft) wide are planted along the north and east walls. In the summer months the colouring, mass and overall pictorial quality of these beds can be appreciated in their full glory.

However, the most remarkable and refined design feature in this garden is probably the western edge of the parterre. Here a 4-metre (13 ft) high retaining wall of light grey granite blocks stretches about 70 metres (230 ft) along the length of the parterre. In the middle it is broken by Italianate steps and at either end is a pretty pavilion with a gently curved slate roof. All along its length the wall is beautifully articulated by a series of short yew hedges placed at right angles to it, like the teeth of a comb (see p. 171). Effectively this hides the wall itself from view, when seen from most angles, and it cleverly breaks up the long horizontal line while at the same time injecting rhythm by means of the vertical hedge elements. The sculptural, spatial and perspective qualities this creates are worthy of comparison with the great masterpieces of European garden design.

As in all great designs, not only is scale handled well, but detail also. Often this only becomes evident on closer inspection. In Pitmedden, for example, one is struck by the beautiful design of the split-pebble paving found near the pavilions, by the steps, in front of the gateway and around the fountain.

Although the parterre garden, or Great Garden, of Pitmedden is the part that rightly attracts most attention, the more restrained designs on the upper level, the entrance level, are also worthy of note. Here a row of pleached limes, two old yew trees, a long hornbeam hedge, a small herb garden, a pergola clad with espalier fruit trees, a circular pond and the gate piers topped with stone pine cones all combine to create a suitable counterpoint to the distinctly colourful parterre garden.

164

170 View across the parterre to one of the two pavilions
at the ends of the long retaining wall.

171 The most notable design feature in the garden is the retaining wall to the west of the parterre garden. The long expanse of wall is beautifully articulated by means of short yew hedges placed at right angles to it.

172 View across the parterre garden to the well-proportioned Italianate steps made of granite masonry. The steps date from the 17th century.

Penshurst Place
A Homage to the Apple Tree

Penshurst was first mentioned in records as far back as the 13th century, and in the course of its 650 years of history, the house has been much altered and extended from de Pultney's original defended manor house. Sir William Sidney was granted the house in 1552 by Edward VI. Successive generations of the Sidney family have used a similar style of architecture in the extension and alteration of the house and gardens.

The basic levels of the garden were laid out in the 16th century by Sir Henry Sidney, including the 106 x 91-metre (350 x 300-ft) plat, which was made by cut and fill, and was probably originally a parterre. Sir Henry's second son Robert, later Earl of Leicester, continued his work by completing the garden walls. The levels laid out in Tudor times survive to this day, and Knyff's 17th-century drawing, later engraved by Kip, bears witness to this. The earldom of Leicester in the Sidney creation ended with the death of the 7th Earl, who had no legitimate male heir, and the house and garden became the property of his niece, Elizabeth Perry. During the 18th century the family found themselves in reduced circumstances and the garden slept whilst elsewhere landscaped parks replaced gardens. Mrs Perry's grandson, Sir John Shelly Sidney (1771–1849), eventually inherited the Estate and began the task of restoring the fabric of the house, continued by his son Philip Charles, 1st Lord De L'Isle and Dudley (1800–51).

Philip, 2nd Baron De L'Isle and Dudley (1828–98) began work on restoring the garden immediately to the south and east of the house. He retained the formal style, which was quite out of step with the fashion for landscape gardens at the time. Penshurst is one of the first examples of the formal

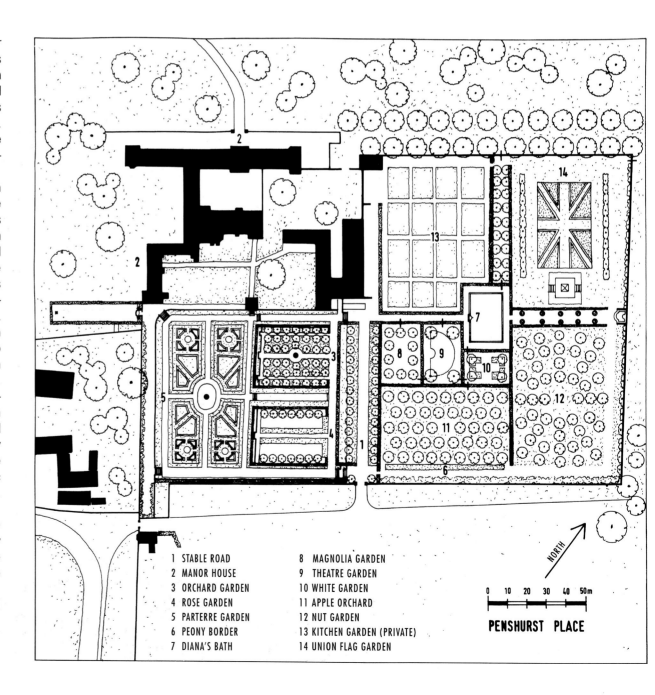

1 STABLE ROAD
2 MANOR HOUSE
3 ORCHARD GARDEN
4 ROSE GARDEN
5 PARTERRE GARDEN
6 PEONY BORDER
7 DIANA'S BATH
8 MAGNOLIA GARDEN
9 THEATRE GARDEN
10 WHITE GARDEN
11 APPLE ORCHARD
12 NUT GARDEN
13 KITCHEN GARDEN (PRIVATE)
14 UNION FLAG GARDEN

NORTH

0 10 20 30 40 50m

PENSHURST PLACE

173 General plan of Penshurst Place in Kent.

174 Apple-blossom time is probably the most important moment in the gardening calendar at Penshurst Place. There are almost 200 apple trees spread throughout the garden.

175 In spring the borders are resplendent with forget-me-nots and wallflowers.

176, 177 Thick yew hedges create a sequence of garden spaces dedicated to different themes. The apple tree is a recurring design feature in all areas of the garden.

178 A grass walk leads the visitor between regularly spaced high yew bushes clipped into hemispherical shapes. At the end of the walk is a small pond.

garden revival of the 19th century. The Elizabethan levels and walls were retained, but yew hedges were planted to divide the gardens into a series of 'rooms', some purely decorative, others vegetable or kitchen gardens. The design is fully in keeping with that of gardens in the 17th century, and when we read in an entry for July 1652 in the diaries of John Evelyn, that he had visited Penshurst 'for its gardens and excellent fruit', we can almost imagine that little has changed down the centuries. Evelyn was referring here to an aspect of Penshurst that is still quite special today: the garden is virtually a homage to the apple tree. The fruit trees were, in fact, planted in the 1930s by Algernon 4th Baron (1855–1945) to generate income, and these standard apples continue to be pruned in the traditional manner, making shapes that break up the outline of the yew hedges.

In 1945 William 1st Viscount De L'Isle VC, KG (1909–91) inherited the house and gardens. During the 45 years he lived at Penshurst he greatly restored and enhanced the gardens, using Lanning Roper and John Codrington for some of the design work. The formal gardens to the east of the garden drive, formerly kitchen gardens, were extended to create a series of garden 'rooms', each of which has a season.

Visitors should follow the brown tourist signs, passing under an archway and following the southern garden wall to turn in to the car park adjacent to the east wall of the garden. The most direct route to the house leads westwards by the lime walk; the garden is entered through a gate in the north-east corner of the wall. Once inside, the visitor should walk southwards. On the walls to the left are espaliered pears and to the right a row of cherry trees, behind which is an enclosure bounded by pleached limes concealing a Union Flag garden, which was opened in May 1986 by HRH The Prince

of Wales; roses and lavender make up the colours of the flag. Continuing southwards one comes to the main axis of the garden from the demi-lune pond; westwards is a view of the house and the hedges frame a fountain. A grass walk leads westwards on the main axis between high hedges to Diana's Bath, a pond with goldfish, lilies and water hawthorn. Wide grass paths lead around the pond and thick, perfectly clipped yew hedges make a clearly defined architectural space.

Leaving Diana's Bath by the south-west corner, one enters a series of smaller gardens, including the White and Gray garden designed by John Codrington, and, westwards, the Theatre Garden, with a small grass amphitheatre. This, in turn, leads to the Magnolia Garden, in the centre of which is a statue of a naiad. Carved around its base is a couplet by Catullus, thought to have been the basis for Sir Philip Sidney's *Astrophel and Stella*; this statue was placed in the garden by the 1st Viscount as a memorial to his first wife Jacqueline, who died in Australia in 1962.

The north-west corner of the magnolia garden leads to a double herbaceous border, at its zenith in late May. Two *Viburnum plicatum* frame the wrought-iron garden gate at the southern end of the garden drive. Continuing on past the Gardener's Cottage, one ascends three steps and turns left, passing first the Spring and Autumn Garden, which is planted with bulbs followed by dahlias and nicotiana. From the garden tower, there is a view of the parterre some 2.5 metres (8 ft) below, with an oval lily pond and fountain in the centre. The four parterre sections framing this pond create a large graphic pattern composed of areas of lawn, box edging and roses. To the west is the narrow church terrace raised by about 2.5 metres (8 ft). In May, the many apple trees form a canopy between the yew hedges; in the distance

are the gentle green hills of the Kent countryside.

Passing along the church terrace and descending to the parterre there is a marvellous view of the south face of the manor house as one walks east, then turns left to enter the rose garden with its beds edged in lavender or Berberis. Descending the steps, once more crossing the herbaceous border, it is worth noticing the long border against the southern wall, where roses are divided into bays by *Bellicent* lilac and, to the left, a magnificent 100m (300ft) peony border, a spectacular sight in June. Behind the peony bed is an apple orchard, which is under-planted with daffodils. The nut garden of Kentish cob nuts under-planted with bulbs of all sorts gives a continuity of colour from spring into early summer. Crab apple trees line the paths to the centre, where a pergola planted with honeysuckle, clematis and roses surrounds a tent-like shape covered with Russian vine. Taking the diagonal path to the north east one returns to the demi-lune and once more looks west across the axis of the garden as Philip 2nd Lord De L'Isle and Dudley conceived it in the latter half of the 19th century.

Reginald Blomfield and Gertrude Jekyll paid tribute to the garden of Penshurst Place as one of the first formal gardens of the 19th century. Evidence from old photographs and paintings shows that the garden has changed little during the 20th century. It is practically a text-book demonstration of how to use walls, hedges, trees and lawns to create garden spaces and then, by means of supplementary elements, to give them a specific theme. Everything is designed with great restraint, but also with great resolution. The concentration on just a few design elements and a rigorous application of the principles of formal garden design make Penshurst Place one of the most rewarding gardens in England.

Hidcote Manor
A Milestone in 20th-Century Garden Design

The gardens presented so far in this book are the result of many years of gradual change and the product of the work of many designers. The garden described here, however, is a completely new creation which makes no reference to previous structures. It was created within the space of 40 years and is the work of a single man, Lawrence Johnston (1871–1958). His wealthy American mother, Gertrude Whitney, purchased the farm of Hidcote Bartrim as an estate and enterprise for Lawrence, her only son by her first marriage. He acquired Hidcote Manor in 1907 and in the seven years leading up to the World War I he laid down all the main parts of the garden as we see it today. Hidcote estate consisted of 280 acres of farmland, with fertile arable land, pasture, woodland and even a tiny hamlet. The garden next to the house was, however, quite small and insignificant. There were one or two fine old trees, including a giant Cedar of Lebanon that we can still admire today, but other than that the site had no proper garden design. In its somewhat windswept position on the crest of a hill in the Cotswolds, the site was not altogether ideal for a garden. Yet here, in the hedge landscapes of Gloucestershire, close to Broadway and Chipping Campden, is one of the most charming stretches of countryside in England. Here we can feel the *genius loci* of an ancient man-made landscape.

Lawrence Johnston was not only a garden designer, but also an excellent connoisseur and collector of plants. He undertook several plant hunting expeditions, including visits to South Africa and China. Many of the plants now nestling in gardens in Europe were discovered and cultivated by him.

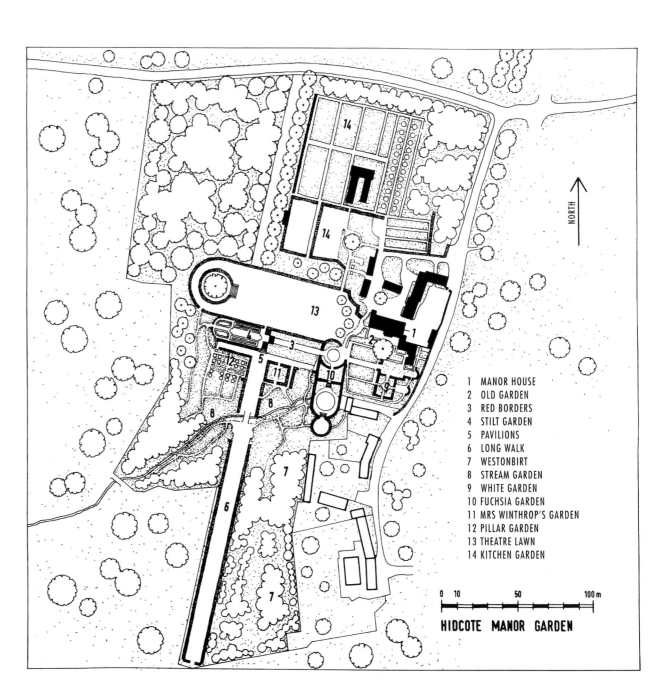

NORTH

1 MANOR HOUSE
2 OLD GARDEN
3 RED BORDERS
4 STILT GARDEN
5 PAVILIONS
6 LONG WALK
7 WESTONBIRT
8 STREAM GARDEN
9 WHITE GARDEN
10 FUCHSIA GARDEN
11 MRS WINTHROP'S GARDEN
12 PILLAR GARDEN
13 THEATRE LAWN
14 KITCHEN GARDEN

0 10   50   100 m

HIDCOTE MANOR GARDEN

180 General plan of Hidcote Manor Garden in Gloucestershire.

181 Close to the house and the splendid old Cedar of Lebanon is the White Garden. Enclosed on three sides by a yew hedge, it is divided into four beds by two paths crossing in the middle. All the flowers planted here are white – white tulips in spring, and white annuals in the summer.

183 The Stilt Garden, a small avenue of square-clipped hornbeam, forms the end of the long axis that starts at the house. An open gate draws the eye to the view of the Cotswolds countryside beyond.

Examples include many decorative shrubs, as well as, most famously, a low-growing, dark-blue lavender known throughout Europe as 'Hidcote Blue'. There is also a low-growing, large-flowered hypericum (St John's wort) called 'Hidcote', a scarlet verbena named Lawrence Johnston, a dark-red pink, *Dianthus* 'Hidcote', a *Campanula latiloba* 'Hidcote Amethyst'. At the beginning of the 1920s Johnston bought himself a second country house near Menton in the south of France. Here, too, he designed a garden and collected subtropical plants. In 1948, at the age of 77, he retired permanently to the south of France, having previously made Hidcote over to the National Trust in 1947.

The main features in the design of Hidcote Manor Garden are the loose structure of hedged enclosures that are thematically quite different and the long sight lines. In *Ancestral Voices*, published in 1975, James Lees-Milne describes a garden that '... is not only beautiful but remarkable in that it is full of surprises. You are constantly led from one space to another, into long vistas and little enclosures, which seem infinite.'[112] Surprisingly there was never an overall plan for the garden – the composition grew instead through the addition of new sections over the period in which the garden was created.

A look at the overall design will reveal that the house itself, a 17th-century manor house, stands quite unobtrusively at the edge of the garden. It does not dominate as does, for example,

Montacute House. Nevertheless, Hidcote Manor is still the hidden key to the whole composition of the garden. One reason for this is that the basic form of a right angle, as prefigured in the plan of the house, recurs again and again throughout the garden. Also, the most important and interesting axis begins at the house, or to be more precise, at the grand old cedar. Following this axis a path leads from this part, the Old Garden, through a circular hedged enclosure to the first highlight along the route, the Red or Scarlet Border. This double border, either side of the beautifully kept grass walk, is planted exclusively with red flowering plants and red foliage bushes. Herbaceous plants, annuals, bulbs and ornamental shrubs grow closely together in this mixed border. It is a demonstration of how the red tones in roses, dahlias, poppies, peonies and the exotic canna lily can be heightened by the proximity of red-leaved acer, ornamental plum, berberis and cotinus.

Two small summer houses or pavilions, flanking a small flight of steps, mark the end of the Red Border and direct the gaze towards the Stilt Garden, a small avenue of square-clipped hornbeam, and to the end of the path, where there is a wrought-iron gate, framed by brick piers. The gate opens onto pasture land dotted with mature trees with the charming Cotswold countryside beyond.

The two pavilions with their up-tilted roof shapes, red brickwork and white-painted lattice windows have become a symbol of Hidcote. This

role derives not only from their distinctive, beautifully proportioned form, but also from their clever positioning in the overall plan of the garden. On the one hand they frame the axis continuing from the Red Border, and on the other, one of the two pavilions is, in quite an unorthodox fashion, the starting point for a second axis, leading off from this point at a right angle. Walking through the small pavilion, one's gaze is directed towards the Long Walk, a grass walk about 200 metres (660 ft) long, bordered by hornbeam hedges, and leading to an open gateway with views across the surrounding countryside.

When walking between the hedges one becomes curious about the parts of the garden hidden behind them. On the east side is the large woodland section that Lawrence Johnston called Westonbirt, probably after an arboretum of the same name created in 1829 near Tetbury in Gloucestershire. In the Westonbirt Arboretum, which is still in existence, there is a wide range of different trees, but Lawrence Johnston's Westonbirt is planted with ornamental shrubs and small trees. Here we find many varieties of ornamental maple, magnolia, ornamental cherry, birch, mountain ash and gingko as well as other, rarer trees and shrubs from China, Japan, Tibet, the Caucasus, Chile and North America. All are grouped together in island beds and make a wonderful display of blossom in spring, and leaf colour in autumn.

Westonbirt leads smoothly into the Stream Garden, a picturesque area laid out as a kind of jungle valley, through which runs a small stream. A greater contrast to the strictly formal design of the Long Walk is hard to imagine, and yet Lawrence Johnston dared to have the Stream Garden cross at a right angle to the walk.

The water course crosses the long, hedge-lined axis, and continues into the lush thicket on the other side. Magnolias, rhododendrons, azaleas, hydrangeas, astilbes, Japanese primroses, many ferns, lilies, bergenias and above all the enormous leaves of the gunnera, a Brazilian member of the rhubarb family, create an almost tropical scene.

Yet all these areas constitute only about half of all there is to see in Hidcote Manor Garden. The visitor continually comes across new areas: the White Garden, the Pillar Garden, with its unusual topiary shapes, and a notable collection of tree peonies, or the Fuchsia Garden surrounded by a mixed hedge of copper beech, holly and yew. Finally, there is also a large kitchen garden, which also contains beds of colourful herbaceous plants.

At the start of the Long Walk is a special part of the garden, called Mrs Winthrop's Garden. It is named after Lawrence Johnston's mother, who lived with her son in Hidcote for over 20 years, and probably designed this part of the garden. Here, in this more or less square hedged enclosure, are flowering plants in shades of golden yellow, cream and white. Here we find thick clumps of Lady's Mantle, evening primrose, hemerocallis, euphorbia and peonies with single, cream-coloured flowers, a variety native to the Caucasus. The golden yellow of the ornamental hop and the complementary spots of dark blue aconite and veronica enhance the overall colour scheme. A few pots of agave lilies, their colourful leaves blending with the rust tones in the paving, give a Mediterranean air.

For the authors of this book, the Theatre Lawn is one of the most beautiful parts of the whole garden. Although many visitors pay it little attention, it is in fact an area of great perfection. Here is an expanse of beautifully level lawn, about 100 by 30 metres (330 by 100 ft) in area and surrounded by a flawless yew hedge. The resulting enclosed space forms an open-air theatre. At the end is a circular 'stage' raised one or two steps above the lawn. In the middle of the stage is a splendid mature beech tree (see Fig. 23). In the summer months plays are sometimes performed in this wonderful setting below the spreading branches of the tree. Even when not used as a stage, it is extremely impressive. The fine old beech and the sea of crocuses and daffodils growing at its feet in spring is itself a natural spectacle. The Theatre Lawn is the largest part of Hidcote Garden, yet a minimum of elements was used in its design. In the same way as the Long Walk it gives strength, grandeur and dignity to the overall composition. Vita Sackville-West used the words 'simple and peaceful' to describe this area.[113]

Hidcote can be described as the most important milestone in garden design in the 20th century. The move away from representative Victorian gardens with their complicated bedding schemes is complete, and all the eclectic ideas that still lent heavy pathos to the garden designs of Reginald Blomfield have vanished. As a result a more intimate scale is regained, such as was so charming in the early Italian Renaissance gardens, and also in the English gardens of the Elizabethan era. An excess of stone structures, which was so often felt to be unsatisfactory in the gardens of Edwin Lutyens, is not at all in evidence at Hidcote. The plantings are the primary design feature, yet they do not obscure the clarity of the structural order. Hidcote is a synthesis of the two diametrically opposed positions of William Robinson and Reginald Blomfield at the end of the 19th century. The formal and the natural, or informal, coexist here in harmony, and the seemingly insurmountable contradiction achieves a striking compositional cohesion. The contradiction heightens and enhances the effect in the individual areas. Vita Sackville-West, whose garden in Sissinghurst was created about 20 years after Hidcote and which is often mentioned in the same breath as the latter, praised 'the nice distinction between formality and informality'[114] and admitted openly, 'There are many lessons to be learnt from it, both for the expert and the amateur.'

184 In contrast to the many strictly formal parts of the garden a number of sections are designed along more informal, picturesque lines. One such is the Stream Garden, with lush planting either side of a small brook. Many botanical delights can be found here. The skilful design is evident in the clear lines, the arrangement of paths and the smooth transitions to open areas.

185 The Theatre Lawn is one of the most beautiful parts of the whole garden. A large, perfectly flat lawn, enclosed by a flawless yew hedge, forms an open-air theatre. At the end of the lawn, raised slightly, is the 'stage', a small circle of grass in the middle of which grows a fine beech tree. Plays are sometimes performed here in summer.
(As previously mentioned, this tree had to be cut down in 1996.)

Hestercombe Garden
A Masterpiece by Edwin Lutyens and Gertrude Jekyll

Hestercombe House, four miles north of Taunton in Somerset, has wonderful views across Taunton Vale towards the Blackdown Hills. In the 18th century the house belonged to the famous landscape painter, Coplestone Warre Bampfylde. As a number of his paintings show, the house was originally designed in the Queen Anne style of the early 18th century, and the garden was laid out as a park.

In the 19th century the property was acquired by Lord Portman, who made the unfortunate decision to redesign the building to fit in with contemporary tastes. As a result the house lost its classical style and became architecturally insignificant. At the south front of the house a large terrace was laid out, with gravel paths and elaborate patterns of bedding plants in line with Victorian tastes. In 1892 the house was given to his oldest grandson, the Honourable E.W.B. Portman, who in 1903 commissioned Edwin Lutyens and Gertrude Jekyll to redesign the garden. The work was completed in 1906. In 1911 Mr Portman died and his widow lived on for another 40 years in Hestercombe House. Following her death the property passed to the Crown Estate Commissioners, who let it to Somerset County Council to house a training and administration centre for the local fire service. Even now, Hestercombe is used in this way. In 1952 all the garden furniture and statuary was auctioned off and the garden was completely neglected for a long time. Not until the end of the 1960s were efforts made to rescue this masterpiece of garden design from oblivion. Research brought to light the original planting schemes and

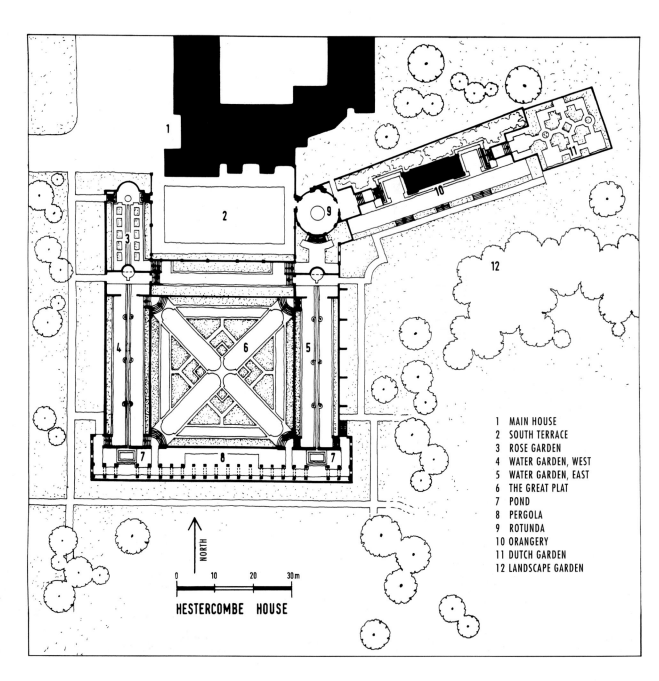

1 MAIN HOUSE
2 SOUTH TERRACE
3 ROSE GARDEN
4 WATER GARDEN, WEST
5 WATER GARDEN, EAST
6 THE GREAT PLAT
7 POND
8 PERGOLA
9 ROTUNDA
10 ORANGERY
11 DUTCH GARDEN
12 LANDSCAPE GARDEN

NORTH

0   10   20   30m

HESTERCOMBE HOUSE

186 General plan of Hestercombe House in Somerset.

187 The centrepiece of the garden is the Great Plat, a
sunken parterre of about 40 metres square (130 ft). Interest
is heightened by the arrangement of two diagonal paths
crossing in the middle.

188,189   Two identically laid-out water gardens flank the east and west sides of the Great Plat. The water springs from a small fountain and flows along a 45-metre (150-ft) long channel to a pond at the end of the garden.

190   View of the Rotunda from the water garden on the east.

184

191 A pergola of about 70 metres (230 ft) long forms the southern end of the parterre garden. The sturdy slate pillars clad with luxuriant roses and clematis mark a distinctive break at the end of the garden and frame the views of the beautiful Somerset countryside.

plans for the overall layout, and the initial phase of replanting was nearing completion.

Lutyens had designed the garden as a terraced parterre, similar to the Italian gardens of the 16th century, like Villa Lante for example. This created a new focal point of the garden below the existing south terrace – the Great Plat, a level area measuring 40 x 40 metres (130 by 130 ft). The contours of the site gave rise to a second area of garden to the east of the Great Plat. Here Lutyens built an orangery and laid out another small parterre garden, the 'Dutch' or East Raised Garden. As this part of the garden is at a slight angle to the Great Plat, Lutyens added a third element, the Rotunda, a circular area of garden, as a transition zone.

The Great Plat is not only designed as a parterre, but also as a sunken garden. The large square section in the middle, interestingly articulated by two diagonal paths crossing in the centre, is surrounded on all four sides by raised sections of garden. In the corners of the sunken garden steps in the form of quarter circles bridge the height difference.

To the east and west the Great Plat is bordered by two identically designed water gardens. Each water feature begins in a small fountain court, enclosed on three sides by high vine- and fig-clad walls. The retaining wall at the front of the court is scooped out like a shell, and at the top of this opening water pours out of the mouth of a stone face into a round pool about 3 metres (10 ft) across. From this pool the water runs into a 45-metre (150-ft) long channel, half a metre (2 ft) wide, along to a rectangular pond at the end of the garden.

At the southern end of the Great Plat and the water gardens is a pergola of about 70 metres (230 ft) long. With its masonry pillars clad with luxuriant climbing roses, vines and clematis, the pergola marks a distinctive break at the end of the garden. At the same time it forms a kind of frame for the views across the beautiful countryside of Somerset.

This ensemble of two water gardens, a sunken garden and the pergola is certainly one of the masterpieces of European garden design. Everything in it speaks of great spatial imagination, formal design skill and a finely developed sense of scale. To reach the second area of garden off to the side, the visitor first has to pass through the Rotunda. This circular space, enclosed within high rubble stone walls, has very decorative paving and a round reflecting pool in the middle.

Steps lead to the orangery. Lutyens designed this building with its classical lines less as a place in which to grow sensitive citrus fruits and more as a summer house or tea house. From the terrace in front of the orangery there is a view of beautiful mature trees that once were a small part of Hestercombe's landscape garden. On the east side of the orangery a few steps lead up to the 'Dutch' or East Raised Garden. This small garden was created on a hill of rubble and stones that was actually intended to be transported away. However, Lutyens saw that this hillock could be used very effectively to create a formal finish to this section of the garden.

In the design of all parts of the garden and also for the orangery and perimeter wall Lutyens used just two types of material – the rough split stone found in the local area and a golden limestone or Ham stone from Ham Hill. All retaining walls and the pillars of the pergola are constructed in this

local slate, with balustrades, some copings and ornamental detail. This achieves a great harmony between the architecture and the natural surroundings.

In the planting scheme for the garden Gertrude Jekyll confined herself to a small range of plants and colours. In restoring the garden the original scheme has been followed as closely as possible. In the sunken garden the first impression of colour, apart from the green of the lawn, is a delicate pink. This shade is enhanced by the strong glossy green of the large-leaved bergenias used to edge all the beds. Other plants growing here include roses, delphiniums and peonies. The main theme in the narrow terrace strips to the north of the sunken garden is shades of grey, supplemented by delicate blue, pink and pale yellow flowers. Here Gertrude Jekyll planted lavender, catmint, thrift, stachys and soapwort. In the rills of the water garden were water lilies, marsh marigolds, forget-me-not, arrowhead and globe flowers. Stronger colours are used in the beds in the water garden on the east side. Here there is a combination of white gypsophila with bright red oriental poppies, blue asters, lavender and globe thistles; also red-hot pokers in shades of orange and yellow, and again and again the deep blue of irises. The planting scheme in the water garden on the west side is quite different. Here there are thick groups of white and orange-coloured lilies, roses, bellflowers and foxglove. The beds are edged with stonecrop, thrift, lilies and bergenia. In other areas of the garden one's eye is constantly drawn by long rows of lavender, rosemary and many grey-leaved plants. Gertrude Jekyll particularly liked stachys, a low-growing plant with furry, silver-grey leaves, excellent for edging.

Snowshill Manor
An Architect's Garden in the Cotswolds

The garden of Snowshill Manor works a special kind of quiet charm on its visitors. It is a quality that is not immediately apparent, but one that grows with each visit.

The varied history of this manor house dates back to the 9th century. Until secularization it belonged to a monastery, and then, in the 16th century it came into the possession of Catherine Parr, the sixth wife of Henry VIII. In the centuries that followed the house changed hands many times, and each new owner made alterations to it. The most significant changes were made in the 1920s by the last private owner, the architect Charles Paget Wade. When, in 1919, at the age of 36, he acquired the house, it was in a dilapidated state. In place of the garden we see today there was just a hillside overgrown with nettles.

Although we have no other evidence of Charles Paget Wade's style, we can assume that, as a famous architect of his day, he had a trained eye for quality in architecture and garden design. In 1910, in the early part of his career, he had worked with Baillie Scott, who was 18 years his senior, at the Hampstead Garden Suburb Trust. There, he also met Edwin Lutyens, who was 14 years older. The rediscovery around 1900 of the Italian Renaissance garden, especially in the English-speaking world, no doubt influenced his design for Snowshill. For are there not certain similarities here to the layout of the garden of Villa d'Este in Tivoli?[115]

192 General plan of Snowshill Manor in Gloucestershire.

193 In around 1920 the architect Charles Paget Wade restored this medieval manor house. On the slope below the house he created a sequence of very impressive small terraced gardens.

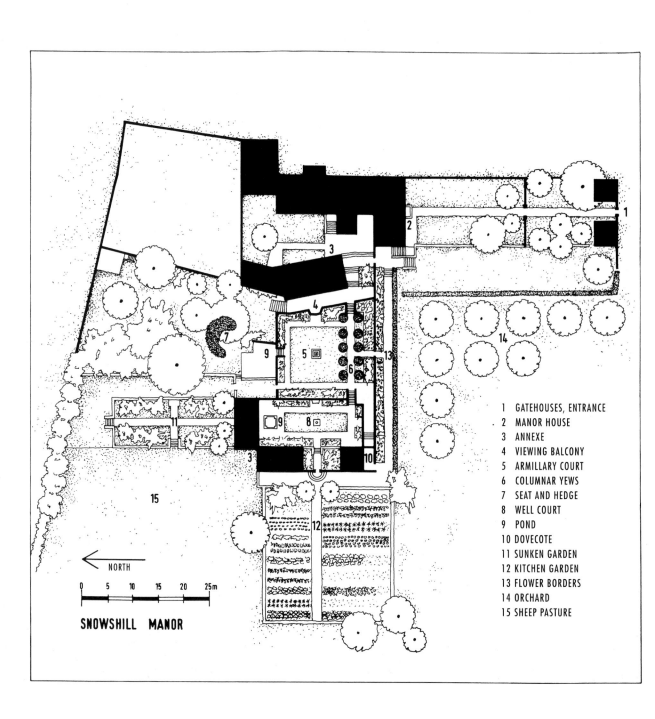

NORTH

0 5 10 15 20 25m

SNOWSHILL MANOR

1 GATEHOUSES, ENTRANCE
2 MANOR HOUSE
3 ANNEXE
4 VIEWING BALCONY
5 ARMILLARY COURT
6 COLUMNAR YEWS
7 SEAT AND HEDGE
8 WELL COURT
9 POND
10 DOVECOTE
11 SUNKEN GARDEN
12 KITCHEN GARDEN
13 FLOWER BORDERS
14 ORCHARD
15 SHEEP PASTURE

194   A box hedge frames this seat under an old ash.

195   The centrepiece of the walled Well Court is a square pond. Placed at the four corners of the pond are blue-painted wooden tubs planted with false cypresses clipped into cones.

196   About 20 metres (65 ft) beyond the main gate is a second garden gate. From here the path emerges from the shade of tall trees into an open area of lawn. Attention is focused on the front door of the house.

197   The path from the house to the garden courts leads down past a double row of large, dark green columnar yews.

198 A view of the Armillary Court, in the middle of which is a gilded armillary sphere, a representation of the celestial sphere.

Charles Wade's financial situation (he owned sugar cane plantations in the West Indies) enabled him to devote his time to his passions, which were architecture, crafts and collecting. Between 1919 and 1923 he restored the manor house and the annexe with great sensitivity and skill. He terraced the surrounding steep hillside in order, as he said, to prevent the house looking as if it were falling into the valley. He had retaining walls built to support the terraces. The walls are made of the same warm grey stone as the house itself, thus creating a harmonious overall picture. In 1951 he gave the entire property, including his extensive collections, to the National Trust. Since that time Snowshill Manor and its garden has been open to the general public.

The entrance to the garden is a gateway framed by two small gatehouses. From here a path leads between tall trees up to another gate. Beyond this is a level expanse of lawn and the main façade of the manor house. On the right, towards the road, is the high perimeter wall, and on the left a low parapet wall, marking the edge of the lawned area, and giving a view of the surrounding hills. When standing in front of the main façade, a small flight of steps then becomes evident on the left. Walking down these steps and round the corner the visitor can then see over the main part of the garden, with its many different, enclosed garden spaces modelled out of the steep hillside.

A narrow gate in the wall leads to the first of these spaces. Above the gate is a small, blue-painted wooden plaque on which Wade inscribed the words:

A gardyn walled with stoon
so fair a gardyn wot I nowhere noon.

A small viewing balcony just below the annexe looks down over this section of garden. High up in the branches of a mighty ash shading the terrace are some Japanese chimes, gently tinkling in the breeze and causing visitors to wonder where the sound is coming from. Below is the Armillary Court, an area of garden with paved paths and modest borders. In the middle of the lawn is a column on top of which is a gilded armillary sphere, a representation of movements of the stars in the celestial sphere, with the Earth in the centre.

A few steps down from the Armillary Court is Well Court, a walled courtyard with a dovecote and outbuildings. Two pretty benches positioned here out of the wind invite one to rest a while. In front of the benches is a small square pond with four false cypresses clipped into cones and placed at the corners. This is a wonderful place to sit and quietly enjoy the view of the pond and beyond it the lawn with its old fountain, to watch the doves flying in and out of the dovecote, and to admire the sundial on the rose- and clematis-clad wall opposite the dovecote. Wade made the sundial himself and placed it here. The clock, and all the wooden parts throughout the property – benches, gates, doors, window frames, panels – are painted in a pretty shade of blue-green. Cotswold connoisseurs call this colour Wade Blue. Wade considered it to be an ideal contrast to the Cotswold stone and the shades of green in the garden.

To the side of Well Court, on the other side of the outbuilding, is a sunken garden, which is turned into a dimly lit, dark green space by the tall thick bushes growing in it. The original plan for the garden shows this area articulated in formal fashion with paths crossing in the middle; it was also a place from which to view the surrounding hills, meadows and woodland. Today it is rather neglected and as a result the design is rather indistinct.

A narrow path leads between the dovecote and one of the outbuildings to a small gate through which is a well-tended kitchen garden.

In order to complete the tour of the garden, the visitor walks along a long, straight path running parallel to the high perimeter wall. Here, in this sheltered spot, is a flower border. On the other side of the path is an orchard.

In its basic design the garden of Snowshill Manor is a match for the famous gardens of Sissinghurst and Hidcote. Here, too, old walls were restored and, step by step, a formal garden built around them.

In the garden of Snowshill Manor (which is only about two acres in extent), the visitor has a strong sense that each space has been very carefully planned. Wade was guided in his design by two principles that he himself devised: 'Firstly, the design of the garden is more important than the plants in it. Secondly a garden must have within it a few secrets and surprises; the visitor should be tempted to look beyond what first meets his eye.'[116] In the garden of Snowshill Manor, therefore, brightly coloured flowers are not what constitutes its charm. Wade deliberately restricted the colours to one range – blues, mauves and purples, all delicately complemented here and there with spots of other colours.

Sissinghurst Castle Garden
A Marriage of Two Minds

English garden design in the 20th century has produced many world-class gardens, the most famous of which, without doubt, is Sissinghurst Castle Garden in Kent, the life's work of the writer Vita Sackville-West (1892–1962) and her husband, the diplomat and writer, Harold Nicolson (1886–1968). They acquired Sissinghurst as a wilderness and transformed it into a luxuriant garden.

Sissinghurst was first mentioned in records dating back to the 12th century. In the 15th and 16th centuries it developed into a substantial estate with a large manor house surrounded by a moat. In the 17th century the property was neglected and for many years it stood empty. Later, during the Seven Years' War (1756–63), Sissinghurst housed French prisoners of war, the walls were fortified, and the manor house became known as a castle, although nowadays there is nothing left of the fortifications. In the 19th century much of the castle was torn down and the few remaining buildings, including South Cottage and the Priest's House, were used as the parish workhouse. At around the turn of the century, Sissinghurst again became a farm. The labourers were accommodated in the tumble-down castle buildings, while the owner built himself a new house in the Victorian style.

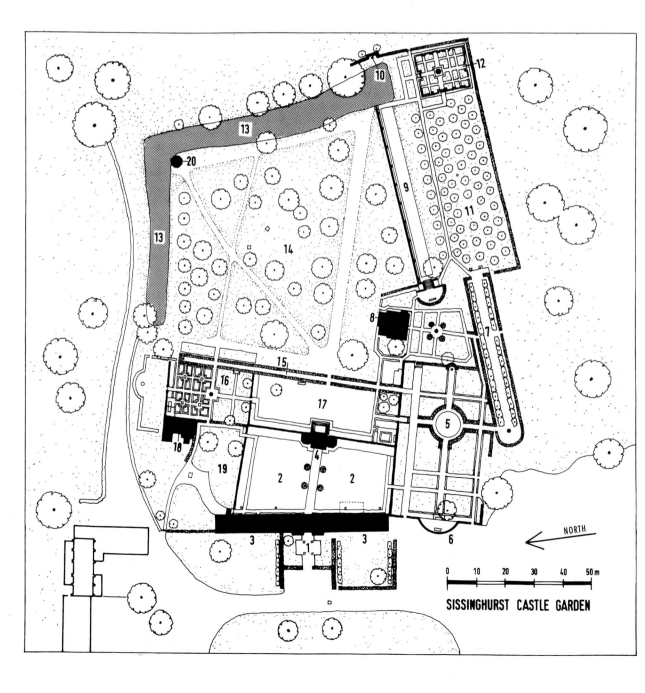

199 General plan of Sissinghurst Castle Garden in Kent: 1 Entrance Court, 2 Lawn, 3 Library, 4 Tower, 5 Rondel in Rose Garden, 6 Private garden, 7 Lime Walk, 8 South Cottage, 9 Moat Walk, 10 Statute of Dionysius, 11 Nuttery, 12 Herb Garden, 13 Moat, 14 Orchard, 15 Yew Walk, 16 White Garden, 17 Tower Lawn, 18 Priest's House, 19 Delos, 20 Gazebo

NORTH

SISSINGHURST CASTLE GARDEN

200 The Priest's House is in the north-west corner of the White Garden.

201 The area of garden in front of the South Cottage is planted exclusively with yellow, orange and red flowering plants. Four columnar yews in the middle provide a vertical element in the composition and give definition.

202 The dark yew hedge is the ideal background for delicate yellow broom.

203 The long axis of the Moat Walk, leading from a raised sitting area to a moat, has banks of azaleas along one side.

In 1930 Sissinghurst was acquired by Vita Sackville-West and Harold Nicolson. They decided to inject new life into the ruin. As there was no longer a manor house as such, and nor was there any intention to reconstruct one, they simply, and unconventionally, split the family up between the various remaining buildings. Vita Sackville-West and Harold Nicolson lived in the South Cottage, which contained their bedroom, the only bathroom on the whole estate and Mr Nicolson's study. The former stables were converted into a library. The tower, a surviving part of the old manor house, was used by Vita Sackville-West as a sitting room and study. Their two sons lived in the Priest's House.

It is perhaps easier to understand why they ventured on this undertaking if we take a look at developments of the time and at the family backgrounds of Harold Nicolson and Vita Sackville-West. Both were members of the privileged classes and had grown up in a period when England was at the height of its power. Each had travelled a great deal in youth, and Vita had often visited Italy, where she got to know the gardens of Florence. In particular she was impressed by the gardens of Villa Gamberaia in Settignano[117] and Villa Medici in Fiesole. As a child, Harold Nicolson had spent a great deal of time abroad, subsequently spending many years in Constantinople, Teheran and Berlin, as a member of the diplomatic service. After his marriage to Vita Sackville-West in 1913, he developed a passion for garden design, an interest that he and his wife shared throughout their lives. Between 1915 and 1930 the Nicolsons gained their first experiences in garden design in the garden of Long Barn, their first home, a converted barn not far from Knole, the family seat of the Sackvilles where Vita had

spent her childhood and youth. However, the hard times suffered by her whole generation as a result of the sweeping changes taking place in society, World War I, and later the shock of the worldwide depression shook the nation's self-confidence. All the traditional values and many social conventions were called into question. It was against this background that Vita Sackville-West and Harold Nicolson sought new ways of making their mark.. In 1930, at the age of 44, Harold Nicolson gave up his secure position in the diplomatic service and turned to journalism, a move that enabled him to fulfil his desire to settle down in England.

In comparison with many others of their class, Vita and Harold Nicolson were not very well off. They were largely reliant on income from their own work to build and maintain their garden. They could not afford a team of gardeners and so it was quite natural for them to do much of the work themselves, although neither had any training in horticulture or garden design. They simply started out as enthusiastic amateurs and learned as they went along. So successful was this method that Vita became a highly respected voice in gardening circles. From 1946 to 1960 she wrote a weekly column on gardening for the *Observer*. Between 1951 and 1958 these collected articles appeared in four volumes entitled *In Your Garden*.[118] Her expertise was so highly regarded that in 1948 she was appointed a member of the newly founded Gardening Committee of the National Trust. In this position she played an important role in the National Trust's new acquisitions and garden renovations.

Vita Sackville-West drew inspiration for all her writings from her own garden in Sissinghurst. The garden was created mostly between 1930 and 1937, but in the 1950s, too, some new sections

were added that contributed much to the overall picture. The structure and the spatial organization of the garden were developed by Harold Nicolson, while Vita designed the planting schemes. They did, however, agree on the main principles of the garden. Vita Sackville-West described their work together in the following words: 'My job was the less important one. Harold designed and I planted. I did succeed in making the garden very pretty with my flowers, but the real praise goes to him, as he drew the lines so surely and so well, that even in winter you can recognise them, when all my flowers have disappeared and the structure becomes visible.'[119] Friends of the family, among them the architect Edwin Lutyens and Albert R. Powys, also contributed one or two ideas. Even now, one can sense that Sissinghurst Garden wasn't created from one grand plan, but evolved steadily over the years.

The garden design has a clear, formal structure. The remains of the castle walls were used as a first fixed point. Accumulated debris and rubbish was cleared from them and some sections rebuilt, using old bricks, to create a sequence of walled gardens. This was not only in keeping with a centuries-old English tradition, but also suited Harold Nicolson's taste for oriental-style garden courtyards and Italian *giardini segreti*. The individual spaces are linked by means of unobtrusive openings in the walls or hedges. Behind each wall there is something new and exciting waiting to be discovered, and a tour of the garden holds many surprises for the visitor. In the centre of the spatial arrangement is the tower with its distinctive silhouette. Now open to visitors, it gives a wonderful view of the garden. From here we can appreciate the relationship of the individual garden spaces to each other, and also the way in which the buildings have been incorporated into the design. It also reveals the garden's wonderful setting amidst the gentle rolling countryside of the Weald of Kent. The irregularly planted orchard that occupies almost half the total site forms a seamless transition between the garden and the surrounding landscape.

The challenge of designing the potentially problematic transition from the formal garden to the freely laid out orchard was met in a particularly skilful way. Instead of placing a simple wall or hedge at this junction, a yew walk was planted, 60 metres (200 ft) long and just 1.5 metres (5 ft) wide (see Fig. 28h). When walking from the Tower Lawn or the White Garden into the orchard, the visitor will be surprised at having first to pass through this long axis running at right angles to his direction of movement. He automatically stops and looks right and left down the hedge walk, to the small statues that catch the eye at the ends of the walk. This very unusual long axis also tells us that its creator was looking to achieve more than just the addition of an arrangement of individual walled gardens. Vita and Harold Nicolson knew and loved the Italian Renaissance gardens with their skilfully composed sequence of spaces, arranged along an axis. It was, therefore, inevitable that in Sissinghurst there should be echoes of Italy, of the splendid Viale delle cento fontane in Villa d'Este,[120] and of the grass walk and exedra in Villa Gamberaia. The Moat Walk seems like a hidden reference to both these Italian gardens. It begins just below an exedra-shaped sitting area and continues along past banks of azaleas in all shades of yellow. A pale-coloured statue of Dionysius catches the eye at the end of the walk, where it stands in front of a hornbeam hedge on the other side of the moat that borders the garden on the north-east.

The exedra-shaped wall and the Rondel in the Rose Garden, the long axis of the Lime Walk and the use of sculptures placed in front of dark yew hedges to catch the eye all remind us of devices used in the design of Italian gardens.[121]

Sissinghurst Garden, however, is much more than just skilfully organized space. The real charm of this garden lies in the fact that the formal structure is overlaid with a richly varied and impressively arranged planting scheme. Harold Nicolson rightly remarked in 1937, 'We have achieved our aim of obtaining a perfect balance between the classical and the romantic, between expectation and surprise.'[122] Each individual area of garden has a particular colour-theme. The borders in front of the library are planted in shades of lilac, violet, mauve and purple. The predominant shades in the Rose Garden are pink, blue and violet. In the Cottage Garden there is a delightful mix of warm creams, yellows and oranges. The wonderful effect of this planting scheme never fails to impress all who see it.

In the past garden design often lay in the hands of architects, painters, poets or even priests; here in Sissinghurst garden design is again, as in the Middle Ages, in the hands of gardeners, but resurrected and enriched as never before. As Peter Coats, the English writer on gardens, wrote in 1963, one year after the death of Vita Sackville-West, 'Only a gardener with the eye of an artist and only an artist with the green fingers of a gardener could have created this unusual garden.'[123]

The absolute highlight of Sissinghurst is the White Garden in front of the Priest's House. This area of garden, divided by low box hedges into beds planted only with white flowers, was created in 1950. The concentration on one colour, white, draws attention to the amazing variety of leaf colours and shapes. But also to the shape of the flowers themselves. The White Garden is at its most impressive on dull days. When it rains, or at dusk, the white of the flowers and the silver grey of the many foliage plants are at their most intense.

In Sissinghurst Castle Garden, which spreads over an area of some 500 square metres (550 yards), a whole cosmos is brought together to form a picture of perfect harmony. Already in the late 1930s it attracted ever-growing numbers of visitors. In 1938 it was included in the National Gardens Scheme (see. p. 218) and opened up to the public on certain days of the year.

Vita Sackville-West died in 1962. As her cousin, Eddy Sackville-West (Lord Sackville, the heir to Knole) wrote: 'People's gardens are apt to die with them, even if the status quo is kept.'[124] Harold Nicolson was never the same after her death; in 1967, one year before he died, Sissinghurst passed to the National Trust and since then it has been open for viewing between April and October each year.

At the beginning of the 1980s the garden was attracting about 100,000 visitors per year. In 1990 this figure had risen to almost 200,000. The Trust attempts to keep numbers down by limiting the opening hours and charging an unusually high entrance fee. Sissinghurst is after all not a large-scale landscape garden where the visitors can disperse easily in the grounds, but is instead a relatively small private garden. Despite all the problems arising from the large numbers of visitors, the garden still maintains its special charm.

204, 205 The indisputable highlight of Sissinghurst is the White Garden in front of the Priest's House. This area, created in 1950, is divided by low box hedges into beds planted only with white flowers.

200

206, 207   The concentration on one colour, white, draws attention to the amazing variety of leaf colours and shapes, and also to the shapes of the flowers themselves. The White Garden is at its most impressive on dull days. When it rains, or at dusk, the white of the flowers and the silver grey of the many foliage plants are at their most intense.

Hazelby Garden
A Garden inspired by Hidcote

Hazelby House, a Victorian mansion a few kilometres south of Newbury in Berkshire, was acquired in 1974 by Martin Lane Fox. In the space of 10 years he completely remodelled the house and garden and transformed it into what is in many ways an exemplary design. The first alterations affected the house itself: the roof storey, complete with its Victorian pointed gables, was removed and replaced by a flat roof and balustrading fitted around the edge of the roof. The effect was to change completely the look of the house. Victorian quirkiness gave way to an altogether brighter, more classical charm.

The approach to Hazelby is along small side roads, past patches of woodland and pasture, through a landscape that at times resembles parkland. Closer to the house the road leads between fields with grazing sheep, over a cattle grid and finally to the entrance gateway, which in May is framed with long rows of pale blue iris.

Behind the gateway, in front of the beautiful east façade of the house, clad with climbing roses and clematis, is a circular gravelled entrance court. In the middle of the courtyard is a circular flower bed with a sandstone vase on a base in the middle. Tall panicles of grass play around the ochre stone, and the yellow tones are taken up in the spurge and rose of Sharon and in a whole variety of yellow-flowering plants. This little ensemble is an early indication of the owner's great experience and sensitivity in grouping plants and of his preference for ordered design and classical statuary.

A small gate at the side of the courtyard leads

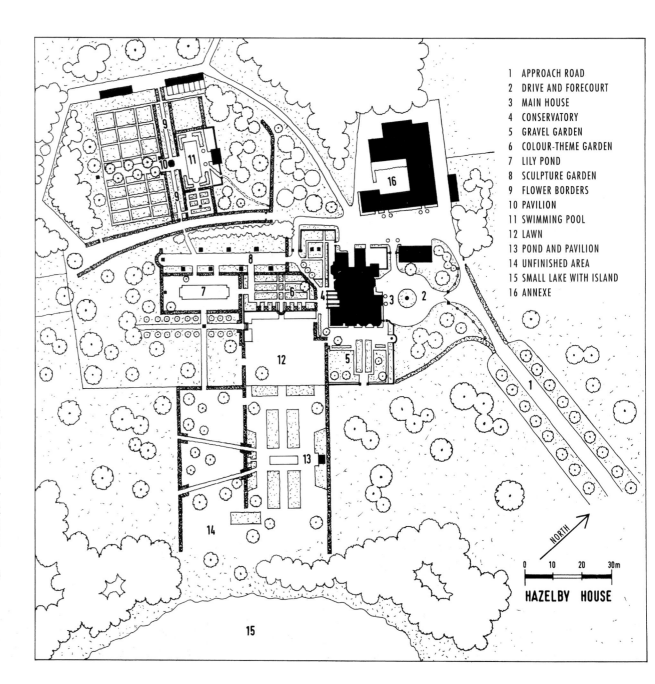

1 APPROACH ROAD
2 DRIVE AND FORECOURT
3 MAIN HOUSE
4 CONSERVATORY
5 GRAVEL GARDEN
6 COLOUR-THEME GARDEN
7 LILY POND
8 SCULPTURE GARDEN
9 FLOWER BORDERS
10 PAVILION
11 SWIMMING POOL
12 LAWN
13 POND AND PAVILION
14 UNFINISHED AREA
15 SMALL LAKE WITH ISLAND
16 ANNEXE

NORTH

0   10   20   30m

HAZELBY HOUSE

208 General plan of Hazelby Garden in Berkshire.

209   When a new owner acquired this Victorian house and garden in 1974, the building itself was the first to be renovated. The entire roof storey, with its Victorian-style pointed gables, was removed and replaced with a flat roof. The roof edge was then finished off with balustrading.

210 A long axis lined with herbaceous borders and hedges leads through the kitchen garden. Halfway along the path is a small pavilion clad with climbing roses.

211 This area of the garden, with its shades of rose, mauve and violet, is almost a homage to Sissinghurst. Even the silver-leaved ornamental pear (*Pyrus salicifolia*), here clipped into rather a cubic shape, is also reminiscent of Sissinghurst.

to the garden in front of the south side of the house. The area immediately next to the house is paved with stone slabs and is used as a patio. Here, parallel with the house's façade, are two narrow flower beds. The remaining area is laid out as a gravel garden with single clumps of plants growing out of a thick layer of gravel. Among the many botanical delights to be found in this part of the garden, one is soon aware of the dominant elements in the planting scheme: lady's mantle (*Alchemilla mollis*) with its beautifully shaped leaves from which dew and raindrops hang like pears and cranesbill (*Geranium pratense*) with its luxuriant violet blue flowers.

A conservatory built on the west side is the focal point of the house in summer. This was the starting point for the redesign of the main garden, begun in 1975.

The first task was to terrace the gentle north–south slope of the garden in this area and to divide it up into individual sections. Retaining walls and small flights of steps were built, all carefully constructed in brick masonry. In one or two places the perimeter walls were replaced or added to in order to create a number of walled sections. The main emphasis, however, was on planting hedges – many hundreds of metres of hornbeam and yew. This gave the garden its spatial framework.

The first part of the garden, which one enters from the small terrace in front of the conservatory, is like a homage to Sissinghurst. The path is a grass walk. On one side of it is a sequence of beds edged with box and planted with white shrub roses, and on the other are beds with pink, mauve and violet-flowering plants. It is not just the colours and the combination with silver-grey foliage plants that is reminiscent of Sissinghurst, but also a number of other details: the cross axis of the garden ends at a silver-leaved ornamental pear (*Pyrus salicifolia*), which was also the tree chosen as a point of interest at Sissinghurst. Finally, another similarity is the beautiful brick paving of the paths and the verdigris-covered copper tub in the middle of the garden.

The area of garden on the west side, one or two steps higher, has a completely different look. Here variety and colour give way to greater restraint. The space is enclosed within precisely clipped yew hedges and laid with a fine carpet of lawn. In the middle is a large rectangular lily pond whose wide paved rim is perfectly level with the lawn. At the end of the long axis through the pond, and contrasting beautifully with the dark green of the hedge, is a marble bust on a pedestal. This whole area of the garden exudes restfulness and elegance.

Two openings in the yew hedge lead to a linear section of garden to the north, also with a grass walk. Lining both sides of the walk are mixed borders and some charming old sculptures. This area is quite different again in design to the two sections described so far. Movement is indicated in its layout as a walk. This juxtaposition of centrally oriented and linear garden spaces, areas of calm and movement side-by-side, is a design principle already seen in Hidcote and Sissinghurst. At Hazelby, Martin Lane Fox shows that he has made a thorough study of these models and that he has skilfully applied the lessons learned elsewhere to the special situation of his own garden.

The kitchen garden, surrounded by a big, old wall, was also redesigned in line with this principle. Leading from the pretty, white-painted gate of the kitchen garden is a long axis accompanied by flower borders and hedges. Halfway along it is a small pavilion clad with climbing roses. One half of the kitchen garden is still used for growing vegetables and berry fruit, but the other has been divided into three new, hedged enclosures. In the middle section is a swimming pool and small summer house. To one side of this is a white garden, a reference to Sissinghurst, albeit not quite so large or rich in variety as its model, and to the other a utilities area alongside the old greenhouses, which are used for growing various cut flowers and pot plants.

The areas at the opposite end of the garden have been redesigned only in recent years. Close to the lily pond a small brick dovecote was built, and beyond it a sandstone pavilion with a rectangular pond in front. A wide strip of lawn bordered with shrub beds leads gently down to a small lake with fine mature trees along its banks. In the shade of the trees are groups of rhododendrons. Views of the surrounding landscape complete the scene.

As in the case of most of the examples shown in this book, Hazelby was not designed by a professional but by an enthusiastic amateur. Although Martin Lane Fox has been involved with gardens for many years, and now designs them professionally, he had no formal training in the subject. However, Hazelby garden is testimony to the fact that the combination of a well-developed sense of style, the ability to design simple, clear structures, imagination and experience when it comes to planting schemes, and finally a deep-rooted passion are the very foundation for every masterpiece of gardening.

212   The box-edged beds, planted with white shrub roses, also awaken associations with Sissinghurst.

213   Precisely clipped yew hedges border this area of garden in the middle of which is a large, rectangular lily pond. The wide sandstone slabs around the pond are laid perfectly level with the lawn.

Barnsley House
A Garden of Our Time

In the village of Barnsley, between Cirencester and Bibury on the edge of the Cotswolds, is Barnsley House, whose garden has attracted much attention in recent years. The house was built in 1697 as a manor house, later becoming a Rectory until 1939 when it was bought by Cecil and Linda Verey. In 1951 they moved out of the house to make way for their son, the architect and architectural historian David Verey and his wife Rosemary. In the 1960s the Vereys began to redesign the garden, and over the following two decades they changed what had previously been an insignificant plot into one of the most beautiful gardens of our time. Rosemary Verey, like Vita Sackville-West before her, has also written books and articles about gardening and garden design, as well as being herself a practitioner of the art in her own garden. She has become a respected figure among English garden experts. Her son, Charles Verey, who now lives in Barnsley House with his family, has made a name for himself as a designer and maker of garden furniture.

The oldest parts of the garden were laid down at the end of the 18th century. The mortared stone wall surrounding the garden also dates from that time.

In the first phase of the design, work concentrated on the south-west facing part of the garden, which makes up the largest area. Here there was already a lawn and, in the background, one or two fine mature trees, plus a yew hedge. This basic picture was enhanced by adding many ornamental trees and bushes. Rosemary Verey chose mainly yellow-leaved trees and those with attractive autumn colouring. This section now has a small

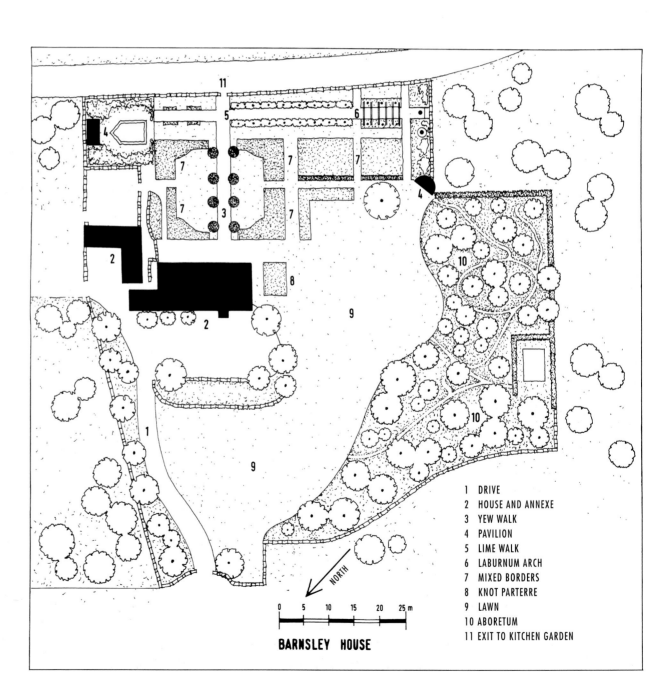

1 DRIVE
2 HOUSE AND ANNEXE
3 YEW WALK
4 PAVILION
5 LIME WALK
6 LABURNUM ARCH
7 MIXED BORDERS
8 KNOT PARTERRE
9 LAWN
10 ABORETUM
11 EXIT TO KITCHEN GARDEN

NORTH

0 5 10 15 20 25 m

BARNSLEY HOUSE

214 General plan of Barnsley House in Gloucestershire.

215 Barnsley House, formerly a presbytery, dates from the 17th century. Its beautiful garden was created only in the last 30 years.

216 The door from the drawing room to the garden. Great care and sensitivity is shown in the choice and grouping of plants.

217 Rosemary Verey, the owner and designer of the garden, has a liking for delicate, muted colours, and for plants with yellow and purple foliage.

arboretum with various types of ornamental cherry, ash, a sequoia, a gingko tree, a trumpet tree, a tulip tree and many others. All are thickly underplanted with bulbs and spring flowering plants, giving interest throughout the year, even before the first buds of spring.

In the second phase of the design, attention focused on the south-east facing part of the garden. When Rosemary and David Verey took over the house the only design feature in this part was a yew walk leading from the garden gate up to the drawing-room door. This axis, lined with beautiful columnar Irish yews, became a main theme in the design and set the tone for the design of the remainder of this section. The overall design here is strictly formal, in contrast to the freer forms found in the south-west facing part. The core of this part of the garden is the lawn around the yew walk and the mixed borders on all four sides. Here, too, Rosemary Verey chose many foliage plants in shades of yellow. In the herbaceous border she preferred delicate, more muted colour tones. At the end of the garden a cross axis intersects – this is the grass walk that continues across the whole width of the site, leading in the north-east corner to a pavilion reminiscent of a classical temple. This small, 18th-century structure used to stand in Fairford Park. In 1962 it was dismantled brick by brick and reassembled in the garden of Barnsley House. The pavilion is reflected in the water of the lily pond just in front of it.

Parallel to the grass walk, a few metres away, is a second cross axis. This walk starts as a lime walk, lined with pleached limes, and continues as a laburnum arch, which can be seen in full blossom at the end of May and the beginning of June.

An interesting feature is the small knot garden that was laid out in 1975 in front of the small loggia on the south-west side of the house. It consists of two square parterres, each measuring 4.5 by 4.5 metres (15 by 15 ft). Rosemary Verey modelled this knot garden on examples taken from the book *La Maison Rustique*, written by Charles Estienne and Jean Libault and published in 1583 and from *The Compleat Gardener's Practice,* written in 1664 by Stephen Blake. The French-inspired knot was planted with box and lavender, the English one with herbs. However, as these herbs all grew at different rates, the pattern never developed into the intended lovers' knot. Therefore, it was replanted using only box. Now both knot parterres have grown to perfection.

In designing the garden of Barnsley House much inspiration came from a study of Hidcote Manor, Sissinghurst Castle and Great Dixter. Russell Page and his work, *Education of a Gardener*, also contributed valuable ideas. At Barnsley, however, the result is not, as at Hidcote and Sissinghurst, an additive structure of individual garden spaces, but more of a continuous smooth sequence of differently designed areas, with graduated transitions between them. Despite the variety of design, everything has a remarkable balance. The relationship between the architectural order and the luxuriant planting is also very well attuned. As at Sissinghurst, the owners themselves were very much involved in the design of the garden. At Barnsley, David Verey was responsible more for planning the overall framework for the design, while his wife concentrated mostly on the planting scheme.

Probably the most notable part of Barnsley House is to be found outside the garden walls. To the south-east of the flower garden, on the other side of a wide unsurfaced path there is a walled kitchen garden newly laid out at the beginning of the 1980s. It is both ornamental as well as useful.

In summer and especially late summer it is a most charming sight. According to David and Rosemary Verey, inspiration for this artistic design came from William Lawson's book *The Country Housewife's Garden* (see p. 20), published in 1617, and the large, reconstructed garden in Villandry.[125] Barnsley House's kitchen garden, measuring about 25 x 25 metres (82 by 82 ft), is not divided into the standard pattern of narrow parallel beds, but comprises a series of geometric patterns, a favourite device of Rosemary Verey. Two main paths crossing in the middle divide the garden into four equal-sized sections. At this centre point is a small square bed planted with ornamental cabbage and lavender bushes, framed by eight, white standard roses. The two halves of the garden, each consisting of two square sections, are laid out as a mirror image of each other. Two of the sections have diagonal axes that produce a pattern of four triangular beds meeting in the centre. In the other two sections paths divide the space into a regular grid, with four smaller beds in the centre, enclosed within L-shaped beds. The delicate grid pattern and geometrical variety is further enhanced by features such as box bushes clipped into balls, or golden privet pyramids marking the corners of the bed. The precisely aligned rows of vegetables and edging plants, including, sometimes, chives and parsley as well as box and lavender, also help underline the basic geometrical pattern. Although all the vegetables are actually quite common varieties they are so impressively grouped that it is hard to imagine how one could ever have thought these plants were unattractive. The delicate, scented green of carrot tops, the grey-green shades of leek or onion plants, the yellow and green of frisée lettuce and the red-brown of oakleaf lettuce have a picturesque charm that is

218 This small 18th-century pavilion, reminiscent of a classical temple, used to stand in Fairford Park. It was dismantled brick by brick in 1962 and erected here in the garden of Barnsley House.

THE ENGLISH FORMAL GARDEN – BARNSLEY HOUSE

hardly less impressive than that of a flower border. The cabbage plants in particular, with their shades of green from grey to blue, are a splendid sight in late summer and autumn. There is beauty, too, in the bizarre, silver-grey leaves of the artichoke, the luxuriant marigold leaves and the crisp leaf shapes of the dwarf bean. Herbs, such as fennel, with its pale yellow umbels, finely fringed dill and borage with its star-shaped flowers in a pretty shade of blue all give added nuances to the overall charming scene.

One of the secrets of the success of this kitchen garden is most certainly the fact that spatial and sculptural factors have not been neglected amidst the sheer delight of designing layouts and plant combinations. Rosemary Verey notes accurately that 'a flat piece of ground is usually dull if it has no element of height'.[126] In her kitchen garden she takes care to provide this element in the form of two small apple trees, but mainly by the use of climbing vegetable plants. Bean-poles and bamboo sticks are arranged into artistically shaped frames for the various kinds of

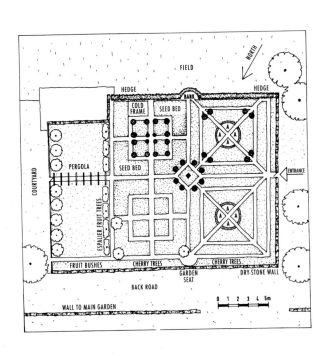

219   Plan of the kitchen garden of Barnsley House.

peas, beans or even sweet peas. A spatial effect is also added by the two wooden lattice arbours, placed at either end of the central path. Decorative hops and vines grow profusely over these arbours thus turning them into distinctive volumes. A further vertical and architectural element is formed by a row of espalier fruit trees, which separate the main part of the vegetable garden from a smaller section at the side. In this part there is a beautiful round-arched pergola, made of metal, used as a frame for growing various different varieties of climbing plants each year – some years there might be runner beans, in others sweet pea or trailing marrows.

Rosemary Verey's kitchen garden is an important development. True, the vegetable garden of Barnsley House is to a certain extent only for show, and often a lettuce, for example, will not be cut because it would otherwise spoil the overall look. However, at the same time it is a model garden. It shows us that the plants we grow for food can also be a great source of nourishment for our sense of beauty.

220 A row of espalier apple trees marks the north side
of the kitchen garden.

THE ENGLISH FORMAL GARDEN – BARNSLEY HOUSE

221 Golden privet and blue-grey cabbages form a very charming colour contrast.

222 The most remarkable part of the garden is the kitchen garden, laid out in 1978. It is both useful and ornamental.

223 This beautiful round-arched pergola made of metal serves both as a vertical and an architectural element. Each year various climbing plants grow up it; in some years there may be runner beans, in others sweet pea or trailing marrow.

A Guide to One Hundred of the Most Beautiful Formal Gardens in the British Isles

The following list of a hundred gardens is an entirely personal selection. It was compiled both to give the reader insight into the basis for the book, and also to serve as a kind of travel guide. It is no exaggeration to say that there is a vast number of gardens worth seeing in England, Scotland and Wales. The authors visited all the gardens between 1985 and 1990, while preparing the German edition of this book. Unfortunately, since this list was first compiled, some of the gardens that we consider among the most beautiful are no longer, or not at present, open to visitors. We continue to list them, nevertheless, and it is always worth checking against the current edition of a good guidebook.

We made use of various guides, first and foremost among them being the National Trust's annual *Handbook*, which lists more than 130 gardens and 250 houses. Founded in 1895 as a private charitable organization with the aim of protecting and preserving the beauty of landscapes and historic buildings the National Trust is now the largest private landowner in Great Britain.

Another guide that we found very useful is *Gardens of England and Wales Open for Charity* (referred to in our listings below as *Gardens Open for Charity*), published by the National Gardens Scheme charitable trust. The 1996 edition lists some 3,500 private gardens. The trust was formed with the aim of making private gardens more accessible to the public, by opening them up on certain days of the year. A small admission fee is charged and the money is donated to various charities.

The *Good Gardens Guide* is also to be recommended. It lists over 1,000 properties in Great Britain and Ireland (1996 edition), the majority of which have gardens well worth seeing. It contains properties owned by the National Trust and also

SCOTLAND

1 Shetland	Tayside)
2 Orkney	7 Stirling (formerly
3 Western Isles	Central)
4 Highlands	8 Fife
5 Moray &	9 Strathclyde[1]
Aberdeenshire	10 East & Midlothian
(formerly	(formerly Lothian)
Grampian)	11 The Borders
6 Angus/Perth/	12 Dumfries &
Kinross (formerly	Galloway

ENGLAND

13 Northumberland	32 Leicestershire
14 Newcastle &	33 Norfolk
Stockton on Tees	34 Hereford &
(formerly Tyne &	Worcester
Wear)	35 Warwickshire
15 Cumbria	36 Northamptonshire
16 Durham	37 Cambridgeshire
17 Newcastle &	38 Suffolk
Stockton on Tees	39 Gloucestershire
(formerly	40 Oxfordshire
Cleveland)	41 Buckinghamshire
18 North Yorkshire	42 Bedfordshire
19 Lancashire	43 Hertfordshire
20 West Yorkshire[2]	44 Essex
21 Humberside[3]	45 Avon[8]
22 Merseyside[4]	46 Wiltshire
23 Greater	47 Berkshire
Manchester[5]	48 London
24 South Yorkshire[6]	49 Somerset
25 Cheshire	50 Hampshire
26 Derbyshire	51 Surrey
27 Nottinghamshire	52 Kent
28 Lincolnshire	53 Cornwall
29 Staffordshire	54 Devon
30 Shropshire	55 Dorset
31 The West	56 West Sussex
Midlands[7]	57 East Sussex

WALES

58 Gwynedd	62 W. Glamorgan[10]
59 Conwy (formerly	63 Mid Glamorgan[11]
Clwyd)	64 Gwent[12]
60 Dyfed[9]	65 S. Glamorgan[13]
61 Powys	

For key to footnotes see opposite

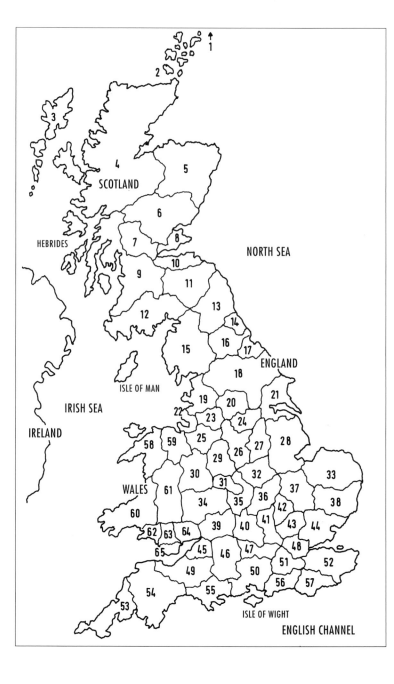

many interesting privately owned estates.

New editions of the three guides mentioned above are published each year and in addition to a description of the property or garden they also contain details of how to get there and the opening times. They can be bought in most bookshops or newsagents. The details of opening times are generally reliable. Most of the properties are open on three to five days a week, usually from lunchtime to early evening.

When visiting the gardens, no one month is better than any other. Between April and October each month has its own particular charms.

From April 1996, county boundaries were changed, as shown below:

1 Glasgow & Edinburgh, North Ayrshire, East Ayrshire, South Ayrshire, South Lanarkshire
2 Bradford, Leeds, Wakefield, Kirklees, Calderdale
3 The East Riding of Yorkshire
4 Liverpool & Manchester
5 Liverpool & Manchester
6 Barnsley, Sheffield, Rotherham, Doncaster
7 Wolverhampton, Dudley, Walsall, Sandwell, Birmingham, Solihull and Coventry
8 From April 1996:NW Somerset, Bath-NE Somerset, City of Bristol, South Gloucestershire
9 Ceredigion, Carmarthenshire, Pembrokeshire
10 Swansea, Neath, Port Talbot, Bridgend
11 Merthyr Tydfil and Rhondda, Cynon, Taff
12 Monmouthshire, Torfaen, Caerphilly, Blaenau Gwent
13 Vale of Glamorgan

ENGLAND

BERKSHIRE

Deanery Garden, Sonning, Berkshire RG4 OUR
Owner: Not known
Viewing: Not available for viewing

In 1901 Sir Edwin Lutyens designed and built a new house in the vernacular style for Edward Hudson, owner of *Country Life* magazine. The garden was also designed by Lutyens and landscaped by Gertrude Jekyll. It is based around an existing orchard, which is the 'wild' garden; the rest of the garden is formal and has been designed to blend with the house, there being courtyards, fountains and lily ponds.

Folly Farm, Sulhamstead, Reading, Berkshire
Owner: The Hon. Hugh & Mrs Astor
Viewing: By appointment
Notes: Recommended

This garden was created in 1901, following plans drawn up by Lutyens. Gertrude Jekyll designed the planting scheme. There is a beautiful water garden, a remarkable sunken garden and many walled gardens. The design is without doubt a masterpiece, but some of the planting is not ideal. See pp. 51, 71, 125.

Hazelby Garden, North End, near Newbury, Berkshire
Owner: Private Trust
Viewing: By appointment
Notes: Not to be missed

This garden was created only in recent years and it has several exemplary formal sections. Stylistically it draws on Sissinghurst Castle garden. Its landscape setting is most charming. See pp. 202ff.

BUCKINGHAMSHIRE

Chenies Manor House, Chenies, Rickmansworth, Hertfordshire WD3 6ER
Owner: Lt Col. and Mrs MacLeod Matthews
Viewing: See *The Good Gardens Guide*
Notes: Recommended

The most beautiful design features of this garden are a fine little sunken garden, a maze, a herb garden and a white garden. Yew hedges and topiary work complete the picture.

Cliveden, Taplow, near Maidenhead, Buckinghamshire SL6 OJA
Owner: The National Trust
Viewing: See the National Trust *Handbook*
Notes: Recommended

This monumental building is fronted by a wide terrace with Italian-style steps. From this point is a view over an extensive parterre garden and beyond it thickly wooded slopes leading down to the Thames. The house is now a luxury hotel.

CAMBRIDGESHIRE

Anglesey Abbey, Lode, Cambridgeshire CB5 9EJ
Owner: The National Trust
Viewing: See the National Trust *Handbook*
Notes: Not to be missed

This extensive estate has both landscaped areas and a number of well-designed formal sections. Special features are the avenue lined with chestnut trees planted in 1937 and various hedged enclosures. In addition there are many examples of well placed statuary. See pp. 43, 110, 112.

CHESHIRE

Arley Hall and Gardens, near Great Budworth, Northwich, Cheshire CW9 6NA
Owner: The Viscount and Viscountess Ashbrook
Viewing: See *Gardens open for Charity*
Notes: Not to be missed

This Victorian country house is surrounded by variously designed garden and park areas. Particularly noteworthy are the double flower-border and an avenue lined with giant ilex topiary.

Little Moreton Hall, near Congleton, Cheshire CW12 4SD
Owner: The National Trust
Viewing: See the National Trust *Handbook*
Notes: Recommended

The 16th-century manor house has beautiful half-timbering. In recent years the National Trust had the gardens redesigned to give the house a suitable setting. One very successful feature of the new design is a small knot garden.

Tatton Park, near Knutsford, Cheshire WA16 6QN
Owner: The National Trust
Viewing: See the National Trust *Handbook*
Notes: Recommended

This Georgian-style house is surrounded by a park of almost 600 acres in area. The splendid tree-lined avenues are particularly impressive. See p. 37.

CUMBRIA

Levens Hall, Kendal, Cumbria LA8 OPD
Owner: C.H. Bagot, Esq.
Viewing: See *The Good Gardens Guide*
Notes: Not to be missed

This Elizabethan manor house has one of the most remarkable topiary gardens in England. Begun at the end of the 17th century, its design has remained practically unaltered to this day.

DERBYSHIRE

Chatsworth, Bakewell, Derbyshire DE45 1PP
Owner: The Duke and Duchess of Devonshire
Viewing: See *The Good Gardens Guide*
Notes: Not to be missed

The castle-like house is surrounded by one of the most beautiful landscape gardens in England. Close to the house are several formally designed areas, including a hedge maze, the winding Serpentine Walk and, in front of the house, a lawn bordered by clipped limes.

Haddon Hall, near Bakewell, Derbyshire
DE45 1LA
Owner: The Duke of Rutland
Viewing: See *The Good Gardens Guide*
Notes: Recommended

This historic manor house is surrounded by terrace gardens with pretty planting schemes and has views over the River Wye and the Derbyshire countryside.

Hardwick Hall, Doe Lea, near Chesterfield, Derbyshire S44 5QJ
Owner: The National Trust
Viewing: See the National Trust *Handbook*
Notes: Not to be missed

This famous Elizabethan mansion house, dating from 1597, has well-designed gardens, which were laid out at the end of the 19th century. A particularly interesting feature is a roughly 120 by 120-metre (395 by 395-ft) area surrounded by high trees and divided into four compartments by hedge-lined alleys. Each quadrant is quite distinct in design, e.g. a kitchen garden, an orchard and a magnolia garden. See p. 135.

DEVON

Castle Drogo, Drewsteignton, near Exeter, Devon EX6 6PB
Owner: The National Trust
Viewing: See the National Trust *Handbook*
Notes: Not to be missed

Castle Drogo was built between 1910 and 1930 to plans drawn up by Sir Edwin Lutyens. George Dillistone, however, devised the planting of the gardens, which with their yew-hedged enclosures are a suitable setting for the house.

Dartington Hall Gardens, Dartington, near Totnes, Devon TQ9 6EL
Owner: Dartington Hall Trust
Viewing: See *The Good Gardens Guide*
Notes: Recommended

The garden plan was drawn up in the 1930s by Beatrix Farrand, an American garden designer. She had previously worked on the design of the garden at Dumbarton Oaks in Washington, USA. Dartington Hall is a masterpiece of modern garden design and displays great confidence in handling scale.

Killerton, Broadclyst, near Exeter, Devon EX5 3LE
Owner: The National Trust
Viewing: See the National Trust *Handbook*
Notes: Recommended

The house dates from the late 18th century and is set in an extensive landscape garden. Close to the house are more rigorously designed areas, including a remarkably well-composed flower border.

Knightshayes Court, Bolham, near Tiverton, Devon EX16 7RQ
Owner: Lady Heathcoat Amory and The National Trust
Viewing: See the National Trust *Handbook*
Notes: Not to be missed

This is one of the most beautiful gardens in Devon. Set in park-like surroundings, the estate has several model examples of formal garden design, with perfect yew hedges, ponds, topiary and statuary. See pp. 113, 131.

DORSET

Athelhampton House Gardens, near Puddletown, Dorchester, Dorset DT2 7LG
Owner: Patrick Cooke Esq.
Viewing: End March–end Oct. Daily (except Sat.) 11.00a.m.–5.00p.m.
Notes: Not to be missed

Set in picturesque landscape in the midst of a large park, the manor house of Athelhampton, built in 1485, has several formal garden sections that bear the hallmark of Inigo Thomas. See pp. 64, 107.

Chantmarle, Frome St Quentin, Dorset
Owner: Privately owned
Viewing: Not open to the public

Inigo Thomas designed the gardens surrounding this Jacobean manor house. Several areas of the garden are very impressive and harmonize extremely well with the medieval building.

Chilcombe House, Chilcombe, near Bridport, Dorset
Owner: Mr and Mrs John Hubbard
Viewing: Wednesday afternoons by appointment
Notes: Not to be missed

This garden, situated by the sea in one of the most beautiful parts of England, was created over the last 25 years. Its intimate scale and unusual colour scheme make it one of the most interesting English gardens of recent times.

Cranborne Manor Gardens, Cranborne, near Wimborne, Dorset
Owner: The Viscount and Viscountess Cranborne
Viewing: See *The Good Gardens Guide*
Notes: Not to be missed

Special attractions in this exemplary design are the yew hedges, perfect lawns, a number of walled gardens, a kitchen garden, an orchard and a knot garden.

Parnham House, Beaminster, Dorset DT8 3NA
Owner: Mr and Mrs John Makepeace
Viewing: See *The Good Gardens Guide*
Notes: Not to be missed

This garden is one of the most beautiful in the whole of Dorset. It is a wonderful example of formal garden design. See pp. 156ff.

GLOUCESTERSHIRE

Abbotswood, Tewkesbury Road, near Stow-on-the-Wold, Gloucestershire
Owner: Dikler Farming Co.
Viewing: As in *Gardens open for Charity* and advertised locally
Notes: Recommended

In 1901 Sir Edwin Lutyens renovated and extended this country house. In the course of this work the garden was also redesigned, in cooperation with Gertrude Jekyll. See Figs. 82, 127, 129.

Badminton House, Badminton, South Gloucestershire GL9 1DB
Owner: The Duke of Beaufort
Viewing: By appointment
Notes: Recommended

Parts of the garden on this enormous estate, dating from the 17th century, were redesigned by Russell Page in 1962. Particularly beautiful parts were created around the Dower House, an ancillary building, and above all in front of the East wing of the main house. Design motifs include flower beds bordered with box, white rose standards, delphiniums, lavender and white-painted pavilions. Sadly, the gardens are not maintained at their best.

Barnsley House, Barnsley, near Cirencester, Gloucestershire GL7 5EE
Owner: Mr and Mrs Charles Verey and Mrs Rosemary Verey
Viewing: See *The Good Gardens Guide*
Notes: Not to be missed

This garden, redesigned after 1960, can be regarded as one of the most beautiful of this century. The kitchen garden is particularly worthy of note. See p. 143 and pp. 208ff.

Eyford House, near Upper Slaughter, Gloucestershire
Owner: Lady Kleinwort
Viewing: By appointment
Notes: Recommended

The house, designed in 1910 by Guy Dawber, is well proportioned and set in formal gardens that merge into the surrounding parkland against a backdrop of beautiful Cotswolds countryside. See pp. 57, 146.

Hidcote Manor Garden, Hidcote Bartrim, near Chipping Campden, Gloucestershire GL55 6LR
Owner: The National Trust
Viewing: See the National Trust *Handbook*
Notes: Not to be missed

With Sissinghurst, probably the most important and influential English garden this century. See pp. 174ff.

Kiftsgate Court, near Chipping Campden, Gloucestershire
Owner: Mr and Mrs J.G. Chambers
Viewing: See *Gardens open for Charity*
Notes: Recommended

Adjacent to Hidcote (see above) this is well worth a visit for the magnificent displays of plants and shrubs and a fine situation and views.

Misarden Park Gardens, Misarden, near Stroud, Gloucestershire GL6 7JA
Owner: Major MTNH Wills
Viewing: See *Gardens open for Charity*
Notes: Recommended

With its splendid yew hedges, wide flower borders, statuary and a terrace overlooking the 'Golden Valley', this private garden on the edge of the Cotswolds is very well worth a visit. See p. 112.

The Priory, Kemerton, Tewkesbury, Gloucestershire
Owner: The Hon. Mrs Healing
Viewing: See *The Good Gardens Guide*
Notes: Not to be missed

The garden is designed on a pleasant, intimate scale and as a result has a very private atmosphere. Its flower borders are among the best in England.

Rodmarton Manor, Rodmarton, Cirencester, Gloucestershire, GL7 6PF
Owner: Mr and Mrs Simon Biddulph
Viewing: See Gardens open for Charity. Groups by appointment.
Notes: Recommended

These gardens are considered to be among the best in Gloucestershire because of their clear overall design. Hedges of hornbeam, ilex and yew mark out areas dedicated to various themes. See p. 141.

Snowshill Manor, Snowshill, near Broadway, Gloucestershire WR12 7JU
Owner: The National Trust
Viewing: See the National Trust *Handbook*
Notes: Not to be missed

Laid out between 1920 and 1923, this very charming garden demonstrates a sure hand in the application of formal design. See pp. 188ff.

Sudeley Castle, Winchcombe, near Cheltenham, Gloucestershire GL54 5JD
Owner: The Lady Ashcombe
Viewing: See *Gardens open for Charity*. Private tours by appointment.
Notes: Recommended

The 12th-century castle stands in exceptionally beautiful surroundings. The most remarkable part of the garden is the parterre with large yew hedges and a centrally placed pond. Its design reveals Elizabethan origins.

Upper Dorval House, Sapperton, Gloucestershire GL7 6LQ
Owner: Not known
Viewing: By appointment
Notes: Recommended

By 1909 this small country house had been created by the Arts and Crafts architect Ernest Barnsley, by adding on to either end of two existing cottages. He laid out a simple garden with yew hedges, topiary work and beds edged with box.

Westbury Court Garden, Westbury-on-Severn, Gloucestershire GL14 1PD
Owner: The National Trust
Viewing: See the National Trust *Handbook*
Notes: Recommended

This garden, which was originally laid out in the style of a 17th-century Dutch water garden, was skilfully reconstructed in the late 1960s. It has canals, yew and ilex hedges and a parterre garden.

HAMPSHIRE

Amport House, near Andover, Hampshire SP11 8BG
Owner: The Ministry of Defence
Viewing: By appointment
Notes: Recommended

The house and garden were redesigned in 1923 following plans by Sir Edwin Lutyens. A terrace bordered by a low balustrade was added in front of the house. From here there is a view across a water garden to the surrounding parkland. The design reveals one of Lutyens's weaknesses – a tendency towards over-complication in the water garden, which has too much stonework. Formal gardens designed by Gertrude Jekyll form an important feature of the estate.

Hinton Ampner Garden, Bramdean, near Alresford, Hampshire SO24 OLA
Owner: The National Trust
Viewing: See the National Trust *Handbook*
Notes: Not to be missed

The house and gardens are situated in a park with stands of fine trees, amidst beautiful surrounding countryside. Close to the house are several formal garden areas bordered with walls and hedges.

King Henry's Hunting Lodge, near Odiham, Hampshire
Owner: The National Trust
Viewing: Not generally open

This garden was started just after World War II and today it is a little-known gem among the properties of the National Trust. John Fowler, a famous designer of textiles and interiors, created the garden for himself. Hornbeam hedges and clipped beech trees leading from the terrace frame the perfectly designed garden in front of this picturesque little house. Summerhouses, sculptures, container plants, a box parterre and flower borders all enrich the general picture. The eye is drawn to a small lake surrounded by splendid trees.

Mottisfont Abbey Garden, Mottisfont, near Romsey, Hampshire SO51 OLP
Owner: The National Trust
Viewing: See the National Trust *Handbook*
Notes: Not to be missed

The history of the house goes back as far as the 12th century. Up until the 16th century it was an Augustinian priory and in the 18th century it was converted into a country house. The most interesting parts of the gardens include a lime walk and a particularly beautiful parterre, which were laid out in the 1930s. The Rose Garden created in the 1970s and 1980s in the walled kitchen garden holds the NCCPG National Collection of old roses. See pp. 41, 85, 87.

West Green House, Hartley Wintey, Hampshire RG27 8JB
Owner: The National Trust
Viewing: See the National Trust Handbook

This 18th-century brick house has some very beautiful and intimate garden areas. Gravel paths, box hedges, small white pavilions and many original details create a charming atmosphere.

HEREFORD AND WORCESTERSHIRE

Conderton Manor, NE of Tewkesbury
Owner: Mr and Mrs W. Carr
Viewing: See *Gardens open for Charity*
Notes: Recommended

Points of interest include the 100-yard long mixed borders, rose walks and formal terrace.

Overbury Court, near Tewkesbury,
Gloucestershire GL20 7NP
Owner: Mr and Mrs B. Bossom
Viewing: See *Gardens open for Charity*
Notes: Recommended

The 1740 Georgian house (not open) is surrounded by landscape gardening of the same date. Formal features include yew hedges and shrub rose borders.

KENT

Godinton Park, near Ashford, Kent TN23 3BW
Owner: Godinton House Preservation Trust
Viewing: By appointment Sunday afternoons, 1st June–30th September, Bank Holidays and Easter holidays
Notes: Recommended

Even though some parts are in the course of restoration, and despite the loss of many fine trees through storms, the garden still has several areas well worth seeing. The yew hedges are unbelievably luxurious.

Great Maytham Hall, Rolvenden, near Tenterden, Kent
Owner: Country Houses Association
Viewing: See *Gardens open for Charity*
Notes: Recommended

Created in 1910 by Sir Edwin Lutyens, the Hall and gardens are a successful blend of fine architecture and garden design. The garden, with its extensive lawns, elegant terrace, beautiful portals and pergola is well kept but today no longer has the breadth of design and lush vegetation typical of its earlier years.

Hever Castle and Gardens, near Hever, Edenbridge, Kent TN8 7NG
Owner: Broadland Properties Ltd.
Viewing: Daily, 1 March–30 November
Notes: Not to be missed

The moated castle dates back to the 13th century and is surrounded by extensive gardens and parkland. Particularly worth noting is the yew maze, which is one of the largest and most beautiful garden mazes in the whole of Europe. Other features are formal, hedged enclosures and an Italian garden with pergolas, water features and sculptures. It was created around 1905 and is an interpretation of Italian garden design, rather exaggerated in scale. New for 1997 is the restoration of the herbaceous border – 110 metres long.

Hole Park, Rolvenden, near Cranbrook, Kent TN17 4JB
Owner: DGW Barham Esq.
Viewing: See *Gardens open for Charity*.

Parties by appointment.
Notes: Recommended

The rhododendrons and azaleas planted in a hollow behind the house form one of the most charming areas of the whole estate. Close to the house are one or two formally designed garden areas, bordered with walls, hedges and topiary work. Christopher Lloyd helped design the excellent planting scheme for the borders.

Penshurst Place, Penshurst, near Tonbridge, Kent TN11 8DG
Owner: Viscount De L'Isle
Viewing: See *The Good Gardens Guide*
Notes: Not to be missed

Penshurst Place, with its hedged enclosures, garden ponds, perimeter walls, flower borders, rows of trees, topiary work and rose parterre, is a classic example of a formal garden. See pp. 168ff.

Sissinghurst Castle Garden, Sissinghurst, near Cranbrook, Kent TN17 2AB
Owner: The National Trust
Viewing: See the National Trust *Handbook*
Notes: Not to be missed

For most visitors to English gardens Sissinghurst is justifiably top of the list. Although often overrun with visitors, it still manages to keep its charm. See pp. 194ff.

The Postern, Tonbridge, Kent TN11 OQU
Owner: David Tennant Esq.
Viewing: By appointment
Notes: Recommended

The garden areas bordered by hedges and walls are very skilfully planted and classical in style. The garden is a recent creation, dating from the 1950s.

NORFOLK

Blickling Hall, Blickling, Norwich, Norfolk NR11 6NF
Owner: The National Trust
Viewing: See the National Trust *Handbook*
Notes: Not to be missed

This is without doubt the most important garden in the county of Norfolk and one of the most remarkable in the whole of England. Its design is clear and extensive in scale. Sadly in recent years storms have badly damaged its trees.

Bradenham Hall, West Bradenham, Thetford, Norfolk IP25 7QP
Owner: Lt Col. and Mrs R.C. Allhusen
Viewing: See *Gardens open for Charity*, or by appointment for groups
Notes: Not to be missed

The main attractions of this 1950s garden are its yew hedges, herbaceous borders, clipped lime trees and arboretum of over 1,000 species, much of which is underplanted with a sea of daffodils.

Felbrigg Hall, Felbrigg, Norwich, Norfolk NR11 8PR
Owner: The National Trust
Viewing: See the National Trust *Handbook*
Notes: Recommended

This garden, exposed to the rigours of a coastal climate, has several very beautiful walled gardens with herb beds and espalier-trained fruit trees.

Oxburgh Hall, Oxborough, near King's Lynn, Norfolk PE33 9PS
Owner: The National Trust
Viewing: See the National Trust *Handbook*
Notes: Recommended

The moated house dates back to the 15th century. Its gardens were created in more recent times and include a parterre, a beautiful flower border and an orchard, which are particularly well worth seeing.

NORTHUMBERLAND

Lindisfarne Castle, Holy Island, Berwick-upon-Tweed, Northumberland TD15 2SH
Owner: The National Trust
Viewing: See the National Trust *Handbook*
Notes: Recommended

In 1903 Lutyens converted the castle into a summer residence for Edward Hulton. Below the castle Gertrude Jekyll created a tiny, skilfully laid out garden with an exemplary planting scheme. High stone walls protect the garden from harsh sea breezes and orientate it towards the fields and meadows.

OXFORDSHIRE

Ashdown House, Lambourn, Newbury, Berkshire RG16 7RE
Owner: The National Trust
Viewing: See the National Trust *Handbook*
Notes: Recommended

Tree-lined avenues cleverly integrate this beautiful 17th-century building into its landscape setting. Sadly the most beautiful avenue was destroyed in a storm in the spring of 1990. See Figs. 26, 82.

Bampton Manor, Bampton, between Witney and Faringdon, Oxfordshire OX8 2LQ
Owner: Earl and Countess of Donoughmore
Viewing: See *Gardens open for Charity*
Notes: Recommended

The garden was designed in the 1950s. Many sections are exemplary. See pp. 57, 99.

Buscot Park, Faringdon, Oxfordshire SN7 8BU
Owner: The National Trust
Viewing: See the National Trust *Handbook*
Notes: Recommended

The gardens at Buscot Park feature a well-designed water axis and a large walled garden. An extensive park and landscape garden provide the backdrop.

Cornwell Manor, Cornwell, near Chipping Norton, Oxfordshire
Owner: The Hon. Peter Ward
Viewing: Not open

This country house, set in charming Cotswolds countryside, has a large kitchen garden and orchard. In front of the living areas of the house is a flower garden, divided into sections by box hedges and topiary work. There is also a water axis and a number of garden sections of freer design. See pp. 126, 127, 146.

Ditchley Park, Enstone, Chipping Norton, Oxfordshire OX7 4ER
Owner: Ditchley Foundation
Viewing: By appointment
Notes: Recommended

In 1933 Sir Geoffrey Jellicoe redesigned parts of the garden near the house as a formal garden. Beyond this is a very beautiful landscape garden. See p. 35.

Garsington Manor, Garsington, near Oxford, Oxfordshire
Owner: Mr and Mrs L.V. Ingrams
Viewing: See *Gardens open for Charity*
Notes: Recommended

Most parts of this attractive country-house garden were created in the 1920s by Lady Ottoline and Mr Philip Morrell. Particularly harmonious sections are the formal pond and the square flower beds accentuated with columnar yews and edged with box.

Pusey House Gardens, Pusey, near Faringdon, Oxfordshire SN7 8QB
Owner: Pusey Estate
Viewing: By appointment only
Notes: Not to be missed

As well as a beautiful landscape garden this estate boasts many formal sections with flower borders, walled gardens and, in front of the house, a large terrace designed by Sir Geoffrey Jellicoe. See p. 111.

SOMERSET

Ammerdown House, near Kilmersdon, Radstock, Bath, Somerset BA3 5SH
Owner: Lord Hylton
Viewing: Bank Holiday Mondays and by appointment
Notes: Recommended

The garden was created in 1902 by Gertrude Jekyll and Sir Edwin Lutyens. The design is strictly formal and has several beautiful areas bounded by yew hedges. Other features include an orangery, fountains, statues and mature trees.

Barrington Court, Barrington, near Ilminster, Somerset TA19 ONQ
Owner: The National Trust
Viewing: See the National Trust *Handbook*
Notes: Not to be missed

This extensive estate consists of an Elizabethan manor house and many farm buildings. There is a very well-tended kitchen garden and, in front of the house, several pretty walled gardens. See Figs. 99, 100, 126, 127.

Barrow Court, near Barrow Gurney, Somerset BS19 3RW
Owner: First Barrow Court Residents Limited
Viewing: By appointment
Notes: Recommended

The garden was designed by Inigo Thomas at around the time that he and Reginald Blomfield wrote *The Formal Garden in England*. It is thus of great historical interest and reveals much of Inigo Thomas's skill in putting his ideas into action.

Brympton d'Evercy, near Yeovil, Somerset
Owner: John Weeks Esq.
Viewing: By appointment
Notes: Recommended

In front of the house's south façade (redesigned in the 17th century) is a beautiful balustraded terrace from which there is a view over a large lawn, perfect flower borders and, in the background, a small lake. The surrounding countryside provides a harmonious setting.

Clapton Court Gardens, near Crewkerne, Somerset
Owner: Mr and Mrs Philip Giffin
Viewing: See *Gardens open for Charity*
Notes: Not to be missed

The garden was created only in recent decades and has several very well-designed sections. In addition to formal areas with yew hedges, ponds and beautiful places to sit, there are also some that are freer in style, for example along the banks of a stream.

Hestercombe Gardens, Cheddon Fitzpaine, near Taunton, Somerset TA2 8LQ
Owner: Somerset County Council
Viewing: See *The Good Gardens Guide*
Notes: Not to be missed

This garden was created around 1906 and recently restored. It is probably one of the most important examples of the work of Gertrude Jekyll and Sir Edwin Lutyens. See pp. 182ff.

Lytes Cary Manor, Charlton Mackrell, near Somerton, Somerset TA11 7HU
Owner: The National Trust
Viewing: See the National Trust *Handbook*
Notes: Not to be missed

The medieval manor house is surrounded by several clearly and simply designed garden areas, forming a harmonious ensemble. See Fig. 102.

Montacute House, Montacute, Somerset TA15 6XP
Owner: The National Trust
Viewing: See the National Trust *Handbook*
Notes: Not to be missed

This wonderful manor house dating from Elizabethan times has one of the finest formal gardens in the whole of England. See pp. 150ff.

Tintinhull House Garden, Farm Street, Tintinhull, near Yeovil, Somerset BA22 9PZ
Owner: The National Trust
Viewing: See the National Trust *Handbook*
Notes: Not to be missed

This garden of this well-proportioned, 17th-century house was created at the beginning of the 20th century by Phyllis Reiss, and, until recently, was tended by the famous gardener, Penelope Hobhouse. The garden is one of the most beautiful in Somerset.

STAFFORDSHIRE

Moseley Old Hall, Fordhouses, near Wolverhampton WV10 7HY
Owner: The National Trust
Viewing: See the National Trust *Handbook*
Notes: Recommended

This small garden is a very pleasing reconstruction in the style of the 17th century. See p. 89.

SURREY

Ham House, Ham, Richmond, Surrey TW10 7RS
Owner: The National Trust
Viewing: See the National Trust *Handbook*
Notes: Not to be missed

The building dates from around 1610 and is surrounded by a garden reconstructed in 1975 according to original 17th-century plans. See p. 91.

Orchards, Munstead Heath Road, Godalming, Surrey GU8 4AR
Owners: Mr Geoffrey Robinson, MP and Mrs Robinson
Viewing: Not open to the public

This country house is one of Sir Edwin Lutyens's finest. The garden was created in cooperation with Gertrude Jekyll. The Dutch garden with its hedged enclosures, rose beds and topiary work is particularly pretty. See Fig. 57.

RHS Garden Wisley, Wisley, near Ripley, Woking, Surrey
Owner: The Royal Horticultural Society
Viewing: See *The Good Gardens Guide*
Notes: Recommended

This 240-acre garden with its wide variety of plants is one of the most important centres of gardening in England. Close to the Edwardian institute building Sir Geoffrey Jellicoe has designed a strictly formal garden with pond, terrace, pergola and rows of trees.

Sutton Place, near Guildford, Surrey GU4 7QV
Owner: The Sutton Place Foundation
Viewing: By appointment
Notes: Recommended

Sutton Place is considered to be one of the most remarkable gardens of the 20th century. It was planned in 1980 by Sir Geoffrey Jellicoe, but only certain sections of the design were carried out. Its rigorous, restrained design and use of modern sculpture show a clear allegiance to the Modern movement.

EAST SUSSEX

Bateman's, near Burwash, Etchingham, East Sussex TN19 7DS
Owner: The National Trust
Viewing: See the National Trust *Handbook*
Notes: Not to be missed

Between 1902 and 1936 this beautiful 17th-century house was the home of Rudyard Kipling, who also designed the garden. With its long rows of clipped limes, yew hedges, walled gardens, flower borders and a lily pond, the garden has an austere beauty. See Fig. 25.

Firle Place, Lewes, East Sussex
Owner: The Viscount Gage
Viewing: See *The Good Gardens Guide*
Notes: Recommended

A beautiful setting at the foot of the South Downs, with views over the parkland. Attractive formal area of Italianate terraces and balustrades.

Great Dixter House and Gardens, Dixter Road, near Northiam, Rye, East Sussex TN31 6PH
Owner: Mr Christopher Lloyd
Viewing: April to mid-October, Tue–Sun, 2.00–5.00p.m.
Notes: Recommended

The 15th-century manor house was renovated and extended by Sir Edwin Lutyens in 1915. The garden was also redesigned at the same time. It contains splendid yew hedges, topiary work and flower borders and has an especially wide variety of plants. See p. 47, 70, 97.

WEST SUSSEX

Heaselands, near Haywards Heath, West Sussex RH16 4SA
Owner: Sir Richard Kleinwort, Bt.
Viewing: By appointment
Notes: Recommended

Parts of the garden, including a pretty sunken garden, were created before World War II; other more freely designed areas were begun in the 1950s. A hollow planted with rhododendrons and azaleas is one of the most impressive parts of the garden.

Little Thakeham, Merrywood Lane, Storrington, West Sussex RH20 3HE
Owner: Mr and Mrs T Ractliff
Viewing: Hotel guests and restaurant visitors only
Notes: Recommended

This small country house, built in 1902 by Sir Edwin Lutyens, is now a hotel. The gardens are worth seeing as an example of an Edwardian country-house garden. The house and garden are surrounded by an orchard and a good time to view is when the apple trees are in blossom.

Nymans Garden, Handcross, near Haywards Heath, West Sussex RH17 6EB
Owner: The National Trust
Viewing: See the National Trust *Handbook*
Notes: Recommended

Only parts of these extensive grounds and gardens are laid out in the formal style. There is a large walled herbaceous garden, topiary work and beautiful old yew hedges. Many of the garden's most precious trees in the Pinetum were lost in the autumn storm of 1987.

Parham House and Gardens, near Pulborough, West Sussex RH20 4HS
Owner: Parham Trust
Viewing: See *Gardens open for Charity*
Notes: Recommended

Fine Elizabethan house set in a beautiful landscape garden. Very impressive flower borders in a large walled garden, formerly the kitchen garden.

WARWICKSHIRE

Packwood House, Lapworth, Solihull, Warwickshire B94 6AT
Owner: The National Trust
Viewing: See the National Trust *Handbook*
Notes: Not to be missed

The Elizabethan house was altered in the 17th century, and many parts of the garden date from this period. These include parts of the famous topiary garden, the mount and a raised terrace-like walk flanked by a flower border. The sunken garden was created much later, around 1930. See Figs. 92, 93, 95.

Upton House, Banbury, Warwickshire OX15 6HT
Owner: The National Trust
Viewing: See the National Trust *Handbook*
Notes: Recommended

The house dates from the 17th century but the garden as we see it today was laid out at the beginning of the 20th century. Rich in diversity, the design includes terraces, flower borders, an orchard and a kitchen garden, as well as several more freely structured areas. See Figs. 51, 52.

WILTSHIRE

Avebury Manor Garden, Avebury, Marlborough, Wiltshire SN8 1RF
Owner: The National Trust
Viewing: See the National Trust *Handbook*
Notes: Recommended

Anyone visiting the megalithic stone circle of Avebury is well advised to take a look at this pretty little garden. A particularly beautiful feature is a winding path with herb beds and topiary work.

The Courts, Holt, near Trowbridge, Wiltshire BA14 6RR
Owner: The National Trust
Viewing: See the National Trust *Handbook*
Notes: Recommended

These gardens, planted in the 1920s, were strongly influenced by the work of Gertrude Jekyll and of Lawrence Johnston at Hidcote. Features include pleached limes, yew hedges and raised terraces.

Hazelbury Manor Gardens, Wadswick, near Box, Wiltshire SN14 9HX
Owner: Not known
Viewing: See *Gardens open for Charity* and by appointment
Notes: Recommended

Grade II formal gardens surround a 15th-century fortified manor house; features include yew topiary, herbaceous and mixed borders and splendid laburnum and beech walkways.

Hillbarn House, Great Bedwyn, Wiltshire
Owner: Mr and Mrs AJ Buchanan
Viewing: See *Gardens open for Charity*. Groups of 10 and over by appointment.
Notes: Recommended

The garden contains some very beautiful hedged enclosures, a hedge tunnel and hedge pavilions. Some of the planting was designed by Lanning Roper at the beginning of the 1960s. The exemplary kitchen garden is especially worth seeing.

Iford Manor Gardens, Bradford-on-Avon, Wiltshire BA15 2BA
Owner: Mrs EAJ Cartwright-Hignett
Viewing: See *Gardens open for Charity*
Notes: Recommended

The romantic terraced garden was laid down before 1914 mostly by the architect Harold Peto. It is a good example of the contemporary English vision of an Italian garden.

Longleat, near Warminster, Wiltshire BA12 7NW
Owner: The Marquess of Bath
Viewing: See *The Good Gardens Guide*
Notes: Recommended

The 16th-century house is set in a large landscape park designed by Capability Brown. The garden areas close to the house were created in the formal style by Russell Page in the 1930s. Features include yew hedges, clipped limes, parterres and statuary. See Figs. 15, 108.

Mompesson House, The Close, Salisbury, Wiltshire SP1 2EL
Owner: The National Trust
Viewing: See the National Trust *Handbook*
Notes: Recommended

When visiting Salisbury cathedral, be sure not to miss this little garden situated very close by. It is an atmospheric town garden with a perfect lawn, flower borders and a wisteria-clad pergola.

Shute House, near Donhead St Mary, Wiltshire
Owner: Mr and Mrs John Lewis
Viewing: Currently closed for extensive renovation. Parties of 15–40 by appointment.
Notes: Recommended

Despite its classical elements of hedged areas, statuary and long water axis the garden is in fact a modern creation. It was designed in the 1970s by Sir Geoffrey Jellicoe and his friends, the owners.

NORTH YORKSHIRE

Newby Hall and Gardens, near Ripon, North Yorkshire HG4 5AE
Owner: R.E.J. Compton, Esq.
Viewing: See *The Good Gardens Guide*
Notes: Not to be missed

Set in extensive parkland the house has several larger areas of formally laid-out gardens with ponds, statuary, flower borders, hedges and a fascinating range of trees. See p. 119.

St Nicholas, near Richmond, North Yorkshire
Owner: The Lady Serena James
Viewing: See *Gardens open for Charity*. Parties by appointment.
Notes: Recommended

This small garden has remarkable yew hedges, topiary and well-composed flower borders.

WALES

GWYNEDD

Bodnant Garden, near Tal-y-Cafn, Colwyn Bay, Clwyd LL28 5RE
Owner: The National Trust
Viewing: See the National Trust *Handbook*
Notes: Not to be missed

The most beautiful garden in Wales. Areas of parkland with rhododendrons, camellias and magnolias are interspersed with formally planned spaces. Splendid yew hedges, an exquisite laburnum arch, ponds, rose gardens and perfect lawns create a wonderful atmosphere. Views over the Welsh countryside round off the picture. See pp. 34, 83.

SCOTLAND

BORDERS REGION

Mellerstain House, near Gordon, Berwickshire, TD3 6LG, Scotland
Owner: The Earl of Haddington
Viewing: See *The Good Gardens Guide*

Notes: Recommended

In 1909 Reginald Blomfield added terraces, flights of steps and lawns to this impressive mansion built in 1770 by Robert Adam.

EAST LOTHIAN

Greywalls, Muirfield, Gullane, East Lothian EH31 2EG, Scotland
Owner: Country-house hotel owned by Giles and Ros Weaver
Viewing: By appointment/visitors to hotel
Notes: Recommended

Situated on the edge of dunes on the Firth of Forth, the house and garden are a masterpiece designed by Sir Edwin Lutyens around 1900. The garden is surrounded by a high wall and has a particular quiet, yet impressive charm. See Fig. 21.

FIFE REGION

Hill of Tarvit, near Cupar, Fife KY15 5PB, Scotland
Owner: The National Trust for Scotland
Viewing: From 1st April–31st Oct: 9.30a.m.–7.00p.m.; from 1st Nov.–30th March: 9.30a.m.–4.00a.m.
Notes: Not to be missed

The house and garden, designed in 1906 by the Scottish architect, Robert Lorimer, form a strikingly beautiful ensemble, set in a perfect landscape of historic and cultural interest. See p. 69.

GRAMPIAN REGION

Pitmedden, Ellon, near Udny, Aberdeenshire, Grampian AB41 OPD, Scotland
Owner: The National Trust for Scotland
Viewing: 1st May–30th September: 10.00a.m.–5.30p.m.
Notes: Not to be missed

Pitmedden is one of the most impressive formal gardens in Scotland. Parts of the gardens date from the 17th century, other elements were added in the course of restoration work. See pp. 162ff.

TAYSIDE REGION

Kinross House, Kinross, Tayside, Scotland
Owner: Sir David Montgomery
Viewing: See *The Good Gardens Guide*
Notes: Not to be missed

Kinross House has one of the most remarkable gardens in Scotland. The overall design is rigorously classical, and it contains flower borders of unique beauty.

Endnotes

1 Victor Zobel, *Über Gärten und Gartengestaltung*, Munich 1906, p. 31

2 Introduction to 'Of Gardens' from *Essays*, Francis Bacon, London 1625

3 Sir Thomas Browne, *Hydrotaphia. Urne Buriall; or, a Discourse of the Sepulchral Urnes lately found in Norfolk*, London 1658, Chapter 5, section 6

4 The development is dealt with very clearly and in depth in *Britain's Natural Heritage* (Philip Colebourn and Bob Gibbons), London 1987

5 John Evelyn, *Sylva – or a Discourse of Forest Trees*, London 1664

6 Statistical Yearbook of 1989, *Agriculture in the United Kingdom*, published by the Ministry of Agriculture, Fisheries and Food, London

7 Philip Coleburn and Bob Gibbons, *Britain's Natural Heritage*, London 1987, p. 52

8 Jan Kip, Leonard Knyff, *Britannia Illustrata*, London 1970, facsimile reprint, London 1984, edited by John Harris and Gervase Jackson-Stops

9 John Tavener, *Certain Experiments concerning Fish and Fruit*, London 1600, quoted in: Sara Midda, *In and out of the Garden*, London 1982, p. 58

10 Jay Appleton, *The experience of landscape*, London 1975, p. 221

11 Günter Mader, Laila Neubert-Mader, *Italienische Gärten*, Stuttgart 1987, p. 143

12 Ibid., p. 54

13 Hermann Muthesius, 'Der geordnete Garten' ('The Ordered Garden'), in *Stadtbaukunst Alter und Neuer Zeit*, no. 21, Berlin 1920, p. 338

14 Gertrude Jekyll, *Wood and Garden*, London 1899, p. 172

15 Lawrence Weaver, *Houses and Gardens by E.L. Lutyens*, London 1913/1990, p. XVIII

16 Reginald Blomfield, Inigo Thomas, *The Formal Garden in England*, London 1892, pp. 1–2

17 Cited in Gavin Stamp, André Goulancourt, *The English House 1860–1914*, London 1986, p. 13

18 This refers to The Deanery, near Sonning in Berkshire, see Lawrence Weaver, *Houses and Gardens by E.L. Lutyens*, London 1913/1990, p. 53ff.

19 Gertrude Jekyll, *Wood and Garden*, London 1899, p. 177

20 Ibid., p. 195

21 John Evelyn, as quoted in: Elizabeth Jane Howard, *Green Shades*, London 1991

22 The inscription is 'Hoc monumentum magno pretio quot aliter in manus publicanorum quandoque cecidisset aedificatum est' (this monument cost a lot of money – money which, sooner or later, would have ended up in the hands of the tax collectors.) See also Jane Brown, *The Art and Architecture of English Gardens*, London, 1989, p. 205, Fig. 31.

23 Hermann Muthesius, 'Der geordnete Garten' ('The Ordered Garden') in *Stadtbaukunst Alter und Neuer Zeit*, no. 21, Berlin 1920, p. 339

24 Thomas Mawson, *The Art and Craft of Garden Making*, London 1900, pp. 207ff.

25 According to statements made by the owner to the authors

26 Gertrude Jekyll, *Garden Ornament*, London 1918/1982, pp. 17, 35

27 Reginald Blomfield, Inigo Thomas, *The Formal Garden in England*, London 1892, p. 102

28 Hermann Muthesius, 'Der geordnete Garten' ('The Ordered Garden') in *Stadtbaukunst Alter und Neuer Zeit*, no. 22, Berlin 1920, p. 358

29 Marie-Luise Gothein, *Geschichte der Gartenkunst*, Jena 1914, vol. 1, pp. 204ff.

30 Günter Mader, Laila Neubert-Mader, *Italienische Gärten*, Stuttgart 1987, pp. 42ff.

31 Jane Brown, *The Art and Architecture of English Gardens*, London 1989, pp. 107, 141. Design for Caythorpe Court (1901) in Lincolnshire and Mellerstain House (1910) in the Borders.

32 Günter Mader, Laila Neubert-Mader, *Italienische Gärten*, Stuttgart 1987, pp. 124ff.

33 Hermann Muthesius, 'Der geordnete Garten' ('The Ordered Garden') in *Stadtbaukunst Alter und Neuer Zeit, no. 22, Berlin 1920, p. 358*

34 Reginald Blomfield, Inigo Thomas, *The Formal Garden in England*, London 1892, p. 12

35 Ibid.

36 Thomas Mawson, *The Art and Craft of Garden Making*, London 1900, p. 65

37 Hermann Muthesius, 'Der geordnete Garten' ('The Ordered Garden') in *Stadtbaukunst Alter und Neuer Zeit*, no. 22, Berlin 1920, p. 358

38 Gertrude Jekyll, *Wood and Garden*, London 1899, p. 84

39 Nancy Mitford, *The Blessing*, London 1951, p. 38

40 This vine was planted in 1768. The stem now has a girth of about a metre and the plant has a spread of more than 40 metres (130 ft).

41 See, for example, *The Studio*, 1903, vol. 34, pp. 135ff. and 1904, vol. 39, pp. 209ff., watercolours by E.A. Rowe and G. Elgood

42 Reginald Blomfield, Inigo Thomas, *The Formal Garden in England*, London 1892, pp. 189–90

43 *The Gardener's Labyrinth* of 1577 contains a number of woodcuts of pergolas. Reproductions can be found in Laurence Fleming, Alan Gore, *The English Garden*, London 1979 and Anthony Huxley, *An Illustrated History of Gardening*, London 1920/1983.

44 Reginald Blomfield, Inigo Thomas, *The Formal Garden in England*, London 1892, p. 190

45 William Robinson, *The English Flower Garden and Home Grounds*, London 1903, p. 132

46 Gertrude Jekyll, *Wood and Garden*, London 1899, pp. 213–14

47 Quoted in Reginald Blomfield, Inigo Thomas, *The Formal Garden in England*, London 1892, pp. 128–30

48 Günter Mader, Laila Neubert-Mader, *Italienische Gärten*, Stuttgart 1987, p. 54

49 Francis Bacon, *Of Gardens*, London 1625

50 William Robinson in the journal *Country Life*, 1912, pp. 410ff.

51 Walter de la Mare, 'The Sunken Garden', *Collected Poems*, London 1994, p. 95

52 Villa Giulia/Rome: see Günter Mader, Laila Neubert-Mader, *Italienische Gärten*, Stuttgart 1987, pp. 23ff. Nymphenbad/Dresden: the authors have not visited these gardens themselves. They refer to the painting entitled *Nymphenbad* by Adolf Menzel in the Kunsthalle in Hamburg.

53 See Josef Kumpan, 'Gartenkunst in Böhmenland' ('Garden Design in Bohemia'), in *Die Gartenkunst*, Munich 1922, p. 21, or 'Garden at Rydal' (Pennsylvania) in *The Studio*, 1902, p. 102

54 Reinhold Hoemann, 'Erinnerungen an die Studienfahrt nach England' ('Memories of a study tour to England'), in *Die Gartenkunst*, Munich 1910, vol. xii, p. 36

55 *Hausgärten – Skizzen und Entwürfe aus dem Wettbewerb Der Woche*, 120- page supplement to the journal *Die Woche*, Berlin 1908, pp. 2, 39, 51, 56, 72

56 Ibid., p. 35

57 Friedrich Ostendorf, *Haus und Garten*, Berlin 1914/1917, pp. 152, 157, 517

58 'Ein Darmstädter Hausgarten' ('Garden of a house in Darmstadt') (Design by the architect Otto

Völkers) in *Die Gartenkunst*, Munich 1917, p. 40

59 Karl Foerster, *Der Steingarten der sieben Jahreszeiten*, Radebeul 1956, pp. 56, 179

60 Gertrude Jekyll, *Wood and Garden*, London 1899, p. 2

61 William Morris, *Hopes and Fears for Art*, as quoted in A.F. Sieveking, *The Praise of Gardens*, London, 1895, p. 303

62 Russell Page, *The Education of a Gardener,* London 1962/1994, pp. 203ff.

63 Künstlerkolonie Mathildenhöhe (Mathildenhöhe Artists Colony) 1899-1914, in: Exhibition Catalogue: *Ein Dokument Deutscher Kunst 1901–1976*, Darmstadt 1977

64 'Garden-Making', in *The Studio*, London 1901, vol. 21, p. 35

65 Francesco Colonna, *Hypnerotomachia Poliphili*, Venice 1499; see Günther Mader, Laila Neubert-Mader, *Italienische Gärten*, Stuttgart 1987, pp. 20ff.

66 Gertrude Jekyll, *Garden Ornament*, London 1918/1982, p. 269

67 Ibid, pp. 269–90

68 Reginald Blomfield, Inigo Thomas, *The Formal Garden in England*, London 1892, pp. 144ff.

69 Inigo Triggs, *Formal Gardens in England and Scotland*, London 1902, p. 211, plate 106, patterns for topiary work

70 Thomas Mawson, *The Art and Craft of Garden Making*, London 1900, pp. 146ff.

71 Edward Prior, in *The Studio*, London 1901, vol. 21, p. 35

72 Francis Bacon, *Of Gardens*, London 1625

73 Hermann Muthesius, 'Der geordnete Garten' ('The Ordered Garden') in *Stadtbaukunst Alter und Neuer Zeit*, no. 22, Berlin 1920, p. 360

74 Francis Bacon, *Of Gardens*, London 1625

75 One of the oldest representations is in the museums at the Vatican: a reclining river god with the attributes of the crocodile and the sphinx to represent the Nile. The river god is surrounded by many cherubic figures.

76 *Country Life* 1908: issue of 11 Jan., pp. 47ff.; issue of 18 Jan., p. 82; issue of 25 April, pp. 590ff.

77 Here the authors have in mind paintings such as *Frühlingsabend* (*Spring Evening*) (1901) by Heinrich Vogeler, *The Acheson Sisters* (1902) by John Singer Sargent, *Mutter und Kind* (*Mother and Child*) (1914) by Hans Unger and *Camargo* (1912) by Gerald Swaish. Also *The Source* (1856) by Jean-August-Dominique Ingres.

78 Inigo Triggs, *Formal Gardens in England and Scotland*, London 1902, p. 57

79 Inscription on a seat designed by Bryant Newbold, see *The Studio*, London 1907, vol. 61, p. 148

80 Gertrude Jekyll, *Garden Ornament*, London 1918/1982, p. 137

81 Ibid., p. 137, pp. 156ff.

82 Reginald Blomfield, Inigo Thomas, *The Formal Garden in England*, London 1892, p. 201

83 Hermann Muthesius, 'Der geordnete Garten' ('The Ordered Garden') in *Stadtbaukunst Alter und Neuer Zeit*, no. 21, Berlin 1920, pp. 337ff.

84 Ibid., vol. 22, p. 360

85 Francis Bacon, *Of Gardens*, London 1625

86 Inigo Triggs, *Formal Gardens in England and Scotland*, London 1902, p. 60

87 Jan Kip, Leonard Knyff, *Britannia Illustrata*, London 1707. Elaborate water pieces can be seen on a number of engravings.

88 Francis Bacon, *Of Gardens*, London 1625

89 The sharp contours are in some cases achieved by sinking slates along the edges of the lawn.

90 John Dando Sedding, *Garden Craft Old and New*, London 1890, p. 150

91 The reference here is to an illustration for *Roman de la Rose* (*The Romance of the Rose*), painted in Flanders in around 1485. This work is now in the British Museum in London (Fig. in: Dieter Hennebo, *Gärten des Mittelalters*, Munich/Zurich 1987, p. 41).

92 Thomas Mawson, *The Art and Craft of Garden Making*, London 1900, p. 149

93 Gertrude Jekyll, *Garden Ornament*, London 1918/1982, p. 189

94 *Guillaume de Machaut sitting in a walled wood*, 1360, illustrated in: John Harvey, *Medieval Gardens*, London 1981, p. 46

95 *Hermitage in a Garden*, c.1400, illustrated in: John Harvey, *Medieval Gardens*, London 1981, p. 7

96 Rudolf Borchardt, *Der Leidenschaftliche Gärtner*, Nördlingen 1987, p. 40

97 As quoted in A.F. Sieveking, *The Praise of Gardens*, London 1885, p. 103

98 Ibid.

99 *Full House* by Molly Keane, London 1986. Quoted in Elizabeth Jane Howard: *Green Shades*, London 1991.

100 Amos Bronson Alcott, *The Garden*, quoted in A.F. Sieveking, *The Praise of Gardens*, London 1885, p. 239

101 A description of the garden of Kenilworth can be found in: Marie-Luise Gothein, *Geschichte der Gartenkunst*, Jena 1914, vol. 2, p. 56

102 Francis Bacon, *Of Gardens*, London 1625

103 William Lawson, *The New Orchard and Garden*, London 1618

104 John Everett Millais, *The Orchard* (illustrated in *The Pre-Raphaelites*, London 1984, p. 172)

105 Reginald Blomfield, Inigo Thomas, *The Formal Garden in England*, London 1892, p. 228

106 Compare, for example, the famous altar painting *Christ in Gethsemane* by the Master of Vyśśí Brod exhibited in St George's Monastery in Prague Castle, or the various paintings of trees in Cerrutti's housebook. Both examples are illustrated in: Gerda Göllwitzer, *Bäume*, Munich 1986.

107 As quoted in A.F. Sieveking, *The Praise of Gardens*, London 1885, p. 104

108 Gertrude Jekyll, *Wood and Garden*, London 1899, p. 181

109 Jane Brown, *The Art and Architecture of English Gardens*, London 1989, pp 128ff.

110 The garden of Barrow Court is documented in *Country Life*, Nov. 1988, pp. 204ff.

111 Günter Mader, Laila Neubert-Mader, *Italienische Gärten*, Stuttgart 1987, p 143

112 James Lees-Milne, *Ancestral Voices*, London 1975, p. 205

113 Vita Sackville-West in *Journal of the Royal Horticultural Society*, vol 74, 11 Nov. 1949

114 Ibid

115 Günter Mader, Laila Neubert-Mader, *Italienische Gärten*, Stuttgart 1987, pp. 140ff.

116 'Snowshill Manor', *The National Trust Guidebook*, London 1965/1988

117 Günter Mader, Laila Neubert-Mader, *Italienische Gärten*, Stuttgart 1987, p. 107

118 Vita Sackville-West, *In Your Garden*, 4 vols 1951–8. New editions of this work have been published several times, most recently in 1986, edited by Robin Lane Fox.

119 Peter Coats, *Famous Gardens*, London 1963, p. 259

120 Günter Mader, Laila Neubert-Mader, *Italienische Gärten*, Stuttgart 1987, pp. 107, 140

121 Ibid, pp. 28, 29

122 Peter Coats, *Famous Gardens*, London 1963, p. 262

123 Jane Brown, *Vita's Other World*, London 1984, p. 131

124 Victoria Glendinning, *Vita*, London 1983, p. 406

125 This is a reference to the Château of Villandry in the Loire Valley. The kitchen garden of Villandry, reconstructed in the 1950s, is one of the most important examples of French garden design.

126 In 1990, when Barnsley House won the Garden of the Year Award, a six-page article was published in the magazine of the London auction house, Christie's.

Select Bibliography

APPLETON, Jay: The Experience of Landscape. London, New York, Sydney, Toronto 1975

BACON, Francis: 'Of gardens'; in: Essays, London 1625

BAILLIE SCOTT, H.M.: Houses and Gardens, London 1907

BLOMFIELD, Reginald, THOMAS, Inigo: The Formal Garden in England, London 1892, 1985 (Reprint)

BORCHARDT, Rudolf: Der leidenschaftliche Gärtner (1938). Stuttgart 1951/1968, Nördlingen 1987

BROWN, Jane: Gardens of a Golden Afternoon, London 1982

BROWN, Jane: The English Garden in our Time – from Gertrude Jekyll to Geoffrey Jellicoe, London 1986

BROWN, Jane: The Art and Architecture of English Gardens, London 1989

BUTLER, A.S.G.: The Domestic Architecture of Sir Edwin Lutyens, London 1950, 1989 (Reprint)

CLAYTON-PAYNE, Andrew: Victorian Flower Gardens, London 1988

CLEVELY, A.M.: Topiary, London 1988

COATS, Peter: Famous Gardens, London 1963

COLONNA, Francesco: Hypnerotomachia Poliphili, Venice, 1499; Facsimile edition, London 1963

COLEBOURN, Philip, GIBBONS, Bob: Britain's Natural Heritage, London 1987

ELGOOD, George Samuel (watercolours), JEKYLL, Gertrude: Some English Gardens, London 1904

ELGOOD, George Samuel: Some Italian Gardens, London 1907

ENKE, Fritz (Editor), MUTHESIUS, Hermann (Editor): 'Hausgärten', supplement to 'Die Woche', Berlin 1907

EVELYN, John: Sylva – or a discourse of forest trees, London 1664

FLEMING, Laurence, GORE, Alan: The English Garden, London 1979

FOERSTER, Karl: Ein Garten der Erinnerung, Leipzig 1950

GORER, Richard: The Flower Garden in England, London 1975

GOTHEIN, Marie-Luise: Geschichte der Gartenkunst, Jena 1914. English edition: A History of Garden Art, London/New York 1928, reissued New York 1966/1979.

GOTHEIN, Marie-Luise: Indische Gärten, Munich, Vienna, Berlin 1926

GRAY, A. Stuart: Edwardian Architecture, London 1985

HAMMERSCHMIDT, Valentin, WILKE, Joachim: Die Entdeckung der Landschaft – Englische Gärten des 18. Jahrhunderts, Stuttgart 1990

HARRIS, John: The Artist and the Country House, London 1979

HARVEY, John: Mediaeval Gardens, London 1981

HENNEBO, Dieter: Gärten des Mittelalters, Munich, Zurich 1987

HOBHOUSE, Penelope: The National Trust Book of Gardening, London 1986

HOBHOUSE, Penelope: Colour in your Garden, London 1985

HÖHLER, Gertrud: Die Bäume des Lebens – Baumsymbole in den Kulturen der Menschheit, Stuttgart 1985

HYAMS, Edward: A History of Gardens and Gardening, London 1971

JEKYLL, Gertrude: Wood and Garden, London 1896/97 as a series of articles in *The Guardian*, 1899 in book form

JEKYLL, Gertrude: Garden Ornament, London 1918, Reprint 1982/1984

JELLICOE, Sir Geoffrey: The Guelph Lectures on Landscape Design, University of Guelph 1983

KNYFF, Leonard, KIP, Jan: Britannia Illustrata, 1707, Reprint 1984, edited by John Harris and Gervase Jackson-Stops for the National Trust

LATHAM, Charles: The Gardens of Italy, London 1905

MADER, Günter: 'How to live with Green'; in 'Stadtbauwelt' 53 24/77, Berlin 1977

MADER, Günter, NEUBERT-MADER, Laila: Italienische Gärten, Stuttgart 1987

MADER, Günter, NEUBERT, Laila: 'Umgang mit Bäumen'; in 'Stadtbauwelt' 64 48/79, Berlin 1979

MAWSON, Thomas: The Art and Craft of Garden Making, London 1900/1912/1926

MASSON, Georgina: Italian Gardens, London, New York 1960

MECKLENBURG, Carl Gregor, Herzog zu: Garten und Landschaft gestern und heute – Zur Geschichte der Gefühle in der Natur, Haigerloch 1984

MIDDA, Sara: In and out of the Garden, London 1982

MUTHESIUS, Hermann: Das Englische Haus – Entwicklung, Bedingungen, Anlage, Aufbau, Einrichtung und Innenraum; (3 volumes, supplement to first volume: 'Development of the garden'), Berlin 1904. English one-volume edition, The English House, reissued 1987.

MUTHESIUS, Hermann: 'Landhaus und Garten'; in 'Dekorative Kunst', page 305 ff. Munich 1907

MUTHESIUS, Hermann: 'Der geordnete Garten'; in 'Stadtbaukunst Alter und Neuer Zeit'. Issue 21, page 337 ff. Issue 22, page 358 ff. Berlin 1920

OLBRICH, Joseph Maria: Neue Gärten von Olbrich, Berlin 1905

OSTENDORF, Friedrich: Haus und Garten, Berlin 1914/1919

OTTEWILL, David: The Edwardian Garden, New Haven and London 1989

PAGE, Russell: The Education of a Gardener, London 1962/1994

PIECHA, Mechthild: 'Auswahl der Stauden mit gestalterischen Augen'; Taspo-Magazin 11/87, Braunschweig

PLUMPTRE, George (Editor): The Latest Country Gardens, London 1988

RAINER, Roland: Gärten, Graz 1982

RAINER, Roland: Lebensgerechte Außenräume, Zurich 1972

ROBINSON, William: The English Flower Garden and Home Grounds, London 1903 and many reprints to 1986

SCHULTZE-NAUMBURG, Paul: Kulturarbeiten Volume II 'Gardens', Munich 1902

SEDDING, John Dando: Garden Craft Old and New, London 1890/1903

SHEPHERD, John, JELLICOE, Geoffrey: Italian Gardens of the Renaissance, three editions: English, French, German, London 1925 and 1953

SOWERBY, John Edward: English Botany, London 1863, 1872, 1886

STAMP, Gavin, GOULANCOURT, André: The English House, London, Boston 1986

TRIGGS, Inigo: Formal Gardens in England and Scotland; Their Planning and Arrangement; Architectural and Ornamental Features, London 1902

WHARTON, Edith: Italian Villas and their Gardens, New York 1903

WIMMER, Clemens Alexander: Geschichte der Gartentheorie, Darmstadt 1989

ZOBEL, Victor: Über Gärten und Gartengestaltung, Munich 1906

Index

Figures in *italics* refer to captions

Picture Acknowledgements

Of the 152 colour pictures in this book, 119 photographs
were taken by the author Günter Mader.

Additional pictures were provided by the following:

Karl-Dietrich Bühler, Genua, Fig. 96, 119, 136, 149, 200,
  215, 220, 223
The Baroness of Earlshall, Leuchars, Scotland, Fig. 103
Hildegard Fuhrer, Fig. 188
E.A. Janes, Berkhamsted, Fig. 8

Knight Frank & Rutley, London, Fig 140
Georges Lévêque, Cloyes-sur-le-Loir, Fig. 98, 152, 191
James Pipkin, Bethesda, Virginia, Fig. 81, 174
Gary Rogers, Hamburg, Fig. 63, 93, 124, 142, 148, 166
Ruprecht Rümler, Cologne, Fig 169
Fritz von der Schulenburg, London, Fig. 91, 190
Bernd Weigel, Baden-Baden, Fig. 19, 58, 83, 147, 160
Parnham Trust, Beaminster, Fig. 163
Malcolm Younger (Knight Frank & Rutley, Edinburgh),
  Fig. 94

Unless otherwise credited, all illustrations are by Günter
Mader, based partly on his own drawings, sketches and
photographs, and partly from old photographs and documents. Site plans were slightly corrected and elaborated
according to locally available plans.

The paintings reproduced on page 23 were kindly supplied
by the Yale Center for British Art in New Haven,
Connecticut. A print of the painting reproduced on page
101 was supplied by Geremy Butler, London.